ALCOHOLISM: THE DISEASE AND THE BENEFITS

Cheri,
    Remember this always.
God has not forgotten you nor
will He ever do this. Our Lord
Jesus loves you and a pain
is never wasted.

Love in Christ
Clayton

ALCOHOLISM: THE DISEASE AND THE BENEFITS

▼

THE HIGHLY EFFECTIVE RECOVERING ADULT-CHILD

LINDA PARKS TAGUE, Ph.D.

Writers Club Press
San Jose New York Lincoln Shanghai

Alcoholism: The Disease And The Benefits
The Highly Effective Recovering Adult-Child

Writers Club Press
an imprint of iUniverse, Inc.

For information address:
iUniverse, Inc.
5220 S. 16th St., Suite 200
Lincoln, NE 68512
www.iuniverse.com

ISBN: 0-595-19902-X

Printed in the United States of America

With Loving gratitude
To the alcoholics in my life…
My father, my son's father,
And my son.

The first two were "constitutionally incapable"
of receiving recovery before their deaths.

My son found the Twelve Steps,
May he keep them!
Thank you, my loves!

CONTENTS

CHAPTER 1

▼

THE TOPIC

The benefits available to the Adult Child of alcoholism are certainly exclusive and somewhat underestimated, if not completely negated! The recovering Adult Child is a very effective and productive member of the work force. I will produce specific case studies to substantiate the unique, energetic and rigorously honest success tactics utilized by this sampling in the workplace. Although their anonymity prevents a history of statistics to support their accomplishments, the humble yet credible and credentialed Adult Child in the professional world can many times out produce their "non-codependent" counterparts.

We hear a lot about how alcoholism is terminal for the alcoholic: but, we do not hear *enough* about the progressive disease of codependency. Recovery means dealing with the entire package of self-defeating, compulsive behaviors. Some recovery professionals suggest these behaviors may have saved our lives. "If we hadn't protected ourselves, we may have given up or developed a fatal illness and died," says Bradford Combs. (1)

The educational trends related to the disease of alcoholism blatantly dictate that it is a disease not unlike diabetes or cancer. The recovery process for those affected by the disease, the statistical five family members for every alcoholic, retorts that we didn't cause this disease, we can't control this disease and we can't cure this disease. The educational trendsetters fail to recognize the very real signs and symptoms exhibited by the families and friends also affected.

Due to the enormous amount of energy expended in trying to cure and control the very progressive and terminal disease of their loved one; the enormous energy expenditures prevents those codependents from realizing their own dreams and goals, the shattered aspirations and hopes caused by the self-sabotage that is also a very real component of this family disease. The educational trends are shifting the spotlight from dependent to codependent awareness. The unresolved issues remain to be the lack of support and understanding in the workplace for the very real and progressive epidemic the loved ones carry, which prevents them from realizing the productive and satisfying careers of which they are more than capable of realizing. The greatest unresolved issues related to education lie not so much upon the shoulders of those affected by the disease as with those responsible CEO's, supervisors and employers who fail to apprise themselves of the ability to support, understand and become willing to mentor the "socio-minority" (11) of codependents striving to realize their greatest potential in the workplace.

The social concerns involved with this willingness are risky. Not unlike the risks involved with hiring the alcoholic, employing the codependent involves taking many risks and involves stretching their capacity for practicing patience, compassion and empowerment. The employee suffering from the effects of loving an alcoholic is often the employee who is frequently absent from the job, who is prone to emotional outbursts of anger, who has difficulty focusing on the

tasks of the day, who is inconsistent with productivity. The social conscience of management must be that of a changed perspective, a new perception of an old problem, a paradigm shift...a powerful "AHA!" experience.

The term "paradigm shift" was introduced by Thomas Kuhn in his highly influential landmark book, *The Structure of Scientific Revolutions.* (2) Kuhn shows how almost every significant breakthrough in the field of scientific endeavor is first a break with tradition, with old ways of thinking, with the old paradigm. The "practicing of principles above personalities", as the Alcoholics Anonymous Big Book suggests, is a tradition for the increased functioning of their groups. Other examples of principles would include integrity and honesty. They create the foundation of trust, which is essential to cooperation and long-term personal and interpersonal growth. Another principle is service or the idea of making a contribution. Another is quality or excellence.

There is the principle of potential, the idea that we are embryonic and can grow and develop and release more and more potential, develop more and more talents. Highly related to potential is the principle of growth...the process of releasing potential and developing talents with the accompanying heed for principles such as patience, nurturing and encouragement. While practices are situational specific, principles are deep, fundamental truths that have universal application. They apply to individuals, to marriages, to families, to private and public organizations of every kind. When these truths are internalized into habits, they empower people to create a wide variety of practices to deal with different situations.

Principles are guidelines for human conduct that are proven to have lasting, permanent value. They are fundamental. One way to grasp the self-evident nature of principle is simply to consider the absurdity of attempting to live an effective life based on their opposites. I doubt that anyone would seriously consider unfairness, deceit, baseness, uselessness, mediocrity or degeneration to be solid foundations for lasting happiness and success.

The more closely our maps or paradigms are aligned with these principles or natural laws, the more accurate and functional they will be. Correct maps will infinitely impact our personal and interpersonal effectiveness far more than any amount of effort expended on just changing our attitudes and behaviors. Changing our attitudes and behaviors can often become the impetus to changing our paradigm and the shift occurs...the beginning of growth, change, new opportunity and success! The double-sided success that attaches itself to both parties involved...even when one party is unaware that the principles have been practiced!

The problem situation or basic difficulty is that of the recurring self-sabotage tactics which result from the decreased self-esteem of the code-pendent. This perpetuates this self-fulfilling prophecy. In order to derail the process, *recovery must be started and continued* to change the faulty thinking patterns.

Recovery is a process. We have heard this countless numbers of times. We have heard this many times because of its truth. Recovery is a process, a gradual one of awareness, acceptance and change. It is also a healing process, yet recovery often feels more like being processed.

Both ideas are true. Recovery is a process by which we change and by which we become changed. The important ideas here are learning when it is time to do something and when it is time just to let something happen.

Although our recovery experiences are unique, there are similarities. Timmen Cermak and other professionals have identified certain recovery stages: survival, denial, re-identification, core issues, reintegration, and genesis. (3) In the pre-recovery stage, denial operates unbidden and we are using our coping behaviors to survive. We do not see things too painful to see; we do not feel emotion too painful to feel. We do not realize our coping behaviors are self-defeating. In fact, we are proud of our gestures. "Look at the people we are taking care of!" We may smile and say, "things are fine," but thing are not fine. We have lost touch with ourselves. We exist, we are not living.

Then something happens. Maybe it's one big problem. Maybe it is several smaller problems or many large ones. Maybe it is the same problem that has happened so many times before. What changes is our reaction. We become fed up. We run out of willpower. We run out of ourselves.

We realize, on some level, that our lives have become unmanageable. Regardless of what the other person is or is not doing, we know our lives are not working. We have been enduring life, not living it. We become *ready* to be changed. Although we may not be sure what, we know something has to change. Something does. We move on to the next stage.

Identification of our behaviors and who we are: instead of taking pride in the coping behaviors, they are seen as self-defeating behaviors. Surrender and acceptance of our powerlessness over other people, other problems, our circumstances, sometimes ourselves and our feelings. We begin to establish a realistic relationship with our strong wills. This stage of recovery can be confusing. We are just recouping from hitting our lowest point. Some recovering people seek professional help at this stage. Some go on antidepressant therapy for a time. Some take jobs beneath their usual level of competence. This can be necessary but frustrating. Our grief work may take much of our energy. Although we have begun recovering we have not yet acquired new living tools.

Now is when we begin experimenting with recovery concepts like detachment, not reacting as much, and letting go. It is time for diligent evaluation of these things we cannot control. It is time for acceptance. In this stage we begin connecting with other people who are in recovery. In this stage we establish or reestablish our relationship with a Higher Power. We begin connecting, or reconnecting, with ourselves.

It is a time to remember that we are more than our pain and more than our problem. It is a time to cling to hope. The healing process has begun. Like healing from very serious invasive surgery, it hurts most the day *after* the surgery.

The purpose of this study is to motivate the tearful Adult Child to seek, to strive, to succeed. To convince the hopeless, helpless "victim" that, in facing and feeling the fears, then proceeding forward one step at a time, we receive the priceless gift of serenity and the open, gaping wounds begin to heal from the inside out. The solutions are simple but they are not easy! It is work, hard work, and painful work. When we get busy, we get better!

I cannot begin to explain how big an impact really participating in a program has on recovery. When codependents first come to the Twelve Step rooms, all they really want is for everyone to help take the pain away. They do not want to know, or want others to know, all the other "stuff." After a few years

In the rooms with the intense continuous obsessions gone, the clarity of thought produces the quest for knowledge, wisdom, and understanding. After a while we discover that feeling better comes first from within ourselves and then from using our newfound reserves to reach out and touch the lives of others. It comes from serving our fellow human beings.

On the following pages are studies of Adult Children who have reached out, perhaps hesitantly at first, but who have nevertheless changed and touched the lives of others. In them can be found encouragement to climb out of the comfort zone, to attempt something you are not certain you can do. In trying, one may be richly rewarded with the discovery of that very special something that helps the pain goes away…recovery.

When I first considered reaching out to others, I might hesitate: didn't I come to recovery to focus on *my* individual experience, to seek *my* own recovery? Wouldn't contributing to the common good just divert me from personal progress? After finally learning to focus on myself, wouldn't helping others distract me from my goal?

It is true that recovery is a personal program, that it encourages us to face our own particular circumstances; but, it is also a program in which each member's recovery is based on a common sharing of experience, strength and hope. The Twelve Steps help to heal individuals but they also help to heal our relationships and help us to work with others.

Practicing the Twelve Steps offers us an opportunity to share our program in the new way. We benefit when we practice gratitude and service is gratitude in action. We acknowledge that we have made progress in recovery, not on our own but with the help of many other members…and through the guidance of Higher Power. In helping others, we drop any pretense that we *alone* are in charge of our separate recoveries. We acknowledge the common bond that unites us in the program and we take steps (however halting and uneven) to align ourselves with the guidance of a Higher Power. By passing on the guidance we have received, we learn a new humility. When we help those who want to be helped, we find new satisfaction in sharing the gift of recovery. We also find that the guidance of a Higher Power is an abundant resource on which we can draw again and again.

The thought of participating in any activity may call up our worst fears of experiencing all over again the criticism, embarrassment, frustration and even despair we have known in the past. Our attempts to help others who grapple with the disease of alcoholism might bring us face to face with the loss of the illusion of control that can result from lending a hand...At first we may experience some discomfort but, we can go at a pace that does not leave us overwhelmed. We are learning and growing at an extraordinary pace.

Sometimes responsibility brings up a fear more disconcerting than that of simply making mistakes: the fear of failure. Alcoholism has given me a high level of creativity, when left to my own devices, to spin fantasies of disaster! What can be learned through service is that others want me to succeed. Certainly my Higher Power is always with me and is always willing to encourage my success. My group, too, supports my efforts. I have also learned that the fall of my group does not rest in my hands but rather in the hands of a Higher Power, who is not I. Help is always available.

What if I volunteered to help out and succeeded? I did not want to feel responsible for the welfare of a group.

What if I began to dominate the affairs of my group or became distracted from my own recovery by attending to business? And might I lose a healthy sense of humility if people started looking to me for guidance? My fear of success sprang from my experience with alcoholism and feeling that doing a job well meant sacrificing my own happiness. I discovered in recovery that my fear of dominance was a good guarantee I would not be domineering and that giving a hand in group affairs furthered my own recovery instead of derailing it.

I also discovered that I could grow in self-esteem without losing humility. I could enjoy making contributions without feeling that I alone could provide the guidance. Most important, in helping others, as in the rest of my program, recovery urged me to let go. Part of extending a hand is eventually letting go and noticing that, when my job is done, there are more hands willing and able to carry on.

There are many questions to be answered or objectives to be investigated when considering whether Twelve Step recovery is really beneficial for a strong-willed survivor from the devastation alcoholism creates. These questions are answered through the process of recovery and the miracles the participants attest to themselves: What commitment am I willing to make?

When I first came to Al-Anon, I hoped, like many other people, to cure the alcoholic. I sat in meetings, listened attentively and learned very quickly. Then I took all the newfound knowledge and left. I went home and told my husband that he was sick, that his problem was not mine, that I was going to have a life whether he was drinking or not. I am sure someone at those meetings mentioned compassion, but I never heard it.

Months later, my husband somehow found his way into a rehabilitation center and the professionals then suggested that I go back to Al-Anon. "But why?" I thought. "I already learned everything they had to teach me." Still, since I would do anything to help my man, I obediently returned to Al-Anon. I attended a beginners meeting, then regular meetings. Someone mentioned that sometimes newcomers took responsibility for making coffee. Determined to be the perfect Al-Anon member, I agreed to prepare coffee for the group and I made a three-month commitment.

So many of those nights I wanted to stay home and take care of my husband. When I was afraid he might drink, or not go to a meeting, when he was in a bad mood and I knew I could make it better, I did not stay home – because I had made a commitment. Since I have always tried to keep commitments, I never missed a meeting. I could not make a commitment to myself, but my first commitment to Al-Anon kept me coming back.

I began to notice that the people in my group appeared happy and content. They seemed to deal with their problems in a different way. I know I wanted what they had, so I tried listening to them a second time. This time my mind stopped racing. For one hour my focus shifted from the alcoholic and I felt calm and peaceful. Eventually I was able to feel moments of peace outside the meeting.

The importance of this book is to present a motivational tool for those unfortunates who believe they are worthless, that their situations are hopeless, that they could never leave a dangerous family situation because they could never make it in the business world or in raising children by themselves. A tool with real case studies of people whose stories are remarkably similar, who were given the gift of courage to risk trusting enough to share their own experiences with each other and to find hope, wisdom and serenity where once only isolation, despair and thoughts of suicide reigned.

The scope of this project involves three years of research into the lives of recovering family members whose lives have been affected by the disease of alcoholism. Three to six hours a week have been spent in Twelve Step meetings listening to the experiences. Seven to ten hours a week have been spent on one-on-one counseling sessions with a group of five of these women. One to two hours daily have been spent reading literature directed to and written about the codependent individuals whose lives have been impacted as a direct result of someone else's drinking. The stories used in the project are anonymous. Their stories are true and relevant but their recovery works predominantly because of the principle that "Anonymity is the spiritual foundation of all their traditions, ever reminding us to place principles above personalities", as the Twelfth Tradition of AI-Anon states. The anonymity will not be broken.

CHAPTER II

▼

REVIEW OF RELATED REFERENCES

The need for this study is to give hope to the "three to five people whose lives are impacted by every alcoholic." These individuals have isolated themselves into a self-fulfilling prophecy that has given credence to the lies they believe about themselves. Through very credentialed and credible authors on this disease, the fellowship of the Twelve Step way of life, the belief in a Power greater than themselves and individual therapy, these wounded warriors are able to find victory over those addictions and obsessions that have paralyzed their efforts to succeed.

My method of research and approach in this project is eclectic in nature. I have a myriad of excellent authors who have given me great awareness in dealing with this disease and the effects on the lives that it touches. I will be referring to many of their revelations and statistics throughout my project.

I have also selected five individuals who have come into my life during the three years of my involvement with the lives of those affected by the disease of alcoholism. I will be relaying their stories both from their individual perspectives and mine, as a "helper."

These case studies, the research data collected, my experience through counseling and my own experiences, strength and hope, shared as a recovering Adult Child, will all serve to produce timely, relevant and significant results in homage to the thousands of courageous individuals who have become willing to

take upon themselves the journey to their spiritual high places marked by rigorous honesty, open-mindedness and hard work. The journey of a thousand miles begins with a single step…then showing up for what it brings.

The written materials gleaned from my project consist of the works of Melody Beattie: *Codependent No More* and *Beyond Codependency* (1) whose works brought codependents out of the closet and made Codependents Anonymous a recovery beginning for many people who knew something was wrong with their lives but did not have a clue about what it was. After my introduction to her books in 1991, my interest and reading time was borderline obsessive with the multiple books I then devoured.

These books will be listed at the end of this work as part of my bibliography. The years from 1991, up to and including this present year 1997, have consisted of a conscious decision to spend no less than one hour a day in prayer and meditation, with journals chronicling the awareness, both from reading the listed books and the documentation from facilitating groups and in guiding through one-on-one sessions. The groups ranged from my own involvement in Twelve Step meetings along with the "helper" therapist context. These sessions averaged four to five hours a week for a three-year period. (At the time of this project these meetings continue, to a lesser degree.)

The notes and journals are voluminous. Many of the stories that will be dissected within these pages have come from my journals. As mentioned earlier, the anonymity will not be broken.

As written in Ecclesiastes by the wisest man of all time, Solomon, "There is no new thing under the sun." (2) The compilations I have offered in this project are no exception. They are, however, my process toward my own success…giving me the one true happiness of being true to myself and my dreams, visions and self-induced goals.

I have learned so very much through books I have read, dissected and assimilated. I have learned so much from the people God has placed in my life during my research.

I have received so many "Ah-ha's" from the spiritual awakenings. I have received so much as a direct result of giving away what I have acquired. The remarkable law of reciprocity (3) is becoming more and more a very integral part of my life: as a child memorizing these scriptures, to the woman of today who has owned them through God's plan of action for my life. I can only hope that God will give me the honor and privilege of carrying this message to others who are still searching for a way of life, which will fill their spiritual vacuum and restore them to sanity and success in their dreams and goals.

CHAPTER III

▼

METHODOLOGY

A description of my approach to this project is predominantly in the form of case studies. These case studies are a random sampling in that they consist of the people who have come into my life during recovery. They are a biased sampling only because they are such a small segment of the recovery community.

My survey methodology will facilitate the bases for the title statement; that the disease of alcoholism can be a benefit because it becomes the impetus creating the gift of desperation which leads to recovery.

In my surveys of the persons with whom I have come into contact in recovery, clear recognition of the miracles in these lives becomes apparent. They are in the process of becoming all they had ever envisioned and dreamed of becoming. They have acquired and are acquiring these fulfillments not at all as they had hoped and planned. They are unanimous in their summation that because it was the alcoholic(s) who drove them to the rooms of recovery, they can say today that they are grateful for the alcoholic(s) in their lives. A statement that before, or in the early days of recovery, would have been clear and complete absurdity!

The case studies will depict the common thread of total unmanageability of the codependent's life prior to recovery. The court dates, the geographic cures, the financial ruin, the inevitable crisis it takes to bottom out the will of the control freak-codependent that believes the illusion that he/she controls this disease.

The broken dreams, broken promises, broken homes and, many times, broken bones are all part of the process to enable a very sick person to come to the realization that he/she must, without reservation, admit he/she is powerless and his/her life is totally unmanageable. When given the precious gift of desperation, that gift removed the protective wall of deception and denial and uncovered all those secrets that kept him/her so very sick.

Once again, anonymity is the key in order for trust to be established. Trust is a very big issue for the participants in my project; therefore, all measures to assure them of anonymity must be utilized.

The limitations to my project are the small sampling and the skewed sampling due to the population coming from the rooms of recovery and/or other health-related fields.

In this research project I proposed to show that the hideous, heinous disease called alcoholism can, and will, be the very impetus that has enabled struggling codependents and/or Adult Children to seek recovery for their shattered, dysfunctional lives. Within this context, I have both experienced and counseled with individuals who proclaim, "I am grateful today for the alcoholic(s)

In my life." Without the disease, the Twelve Step way of life would never have been discovered. This "way of life" brings serenity, healthy choices and success in all their affairs.

The disease has a double edge and truly has its *benefits* with the above-stated perspectives.

CHAPTER IV

▼

HOW IT WORKS

The American Medical Association recognizes alcoholism as a disease, which can be arrested but not cured. One of the symptoms is an uncontrollable desire to drink. An alcoholic is someone whose drinking causes a continuous or growing problem in any aspect of his or her life. If the alcoholic continues to drink, the compulsion to drink will get worse. The only method of arresting alcoholism is total abstinence. Most authorities agree that, even after years of sobriety, alcoholics can never again control their drinking.

All kinds of people are alcoholics. Most have families, friends and jobs. They function fairly well, but their drinking affects some part of their lives, whether socially, in the workplace, or within their families. Often all three areas are affected to some extent.

There are many successful treatments for alcoholism today. Alcoholics Anonymous is the most well known and is widely regarded as the most effective. It is the nature of the disease that its victims do not believe they are ill. Therefore, hope for recovery lies in their ability to recognize the need for help, their desire to stop drinking and their willingness to enter a program of recovery such as Alcoholics Anonymous.

It is no longer possible to consider alcoholism as a disease affecting only the alcoholic. Others in the family react to the illness. There is considerable evidence that it has disturbing effects on the personalities of family members and family studies indicate that a minimum of one other relative is directly involved.

The relationship between the alcoholic and the family is not a one-way relationship. The family also affects the alcoholic and his or her illness. (The very existence of family ties is related to recovery from alcoholism.) Some families are successful in helping the alcoholic member to recognize a need for help and support treatment efforts. Others may discourage the alcoholic from seeking treatment and may actually encourage persistence of the illness. It is now believed that "the most successful treatment of alcoholism involves helping both the alcoholic and those members of the family who are directly involved in the Alcoholic's behavior". (1)

When two or more persons live together over a period of time, patterns of relating to one another evolve. In a family, a division of function occurs and roles interlock. For the family to function smoothly, each person must plan an appropriate role in a predictable manner. When a family as a whole is functioning smoothly, individual members also tend to function well. Everyone is aware of where he or she fits in, of what is expected and of what, in turn, can be expected from others. When this organization is disrupted, each family member feels repercussions and a crisis is underway.

Family crises often follow a similar pattern, regardless of what may have precipitated them. Frequently there is an initial denial that a problem exists. The family tries to continue its usual behavior patterns until it is obvious that these patterns are no longer effective. At this point there is a downward slump in organization. Roles are played with less enthusiasm and there is an increase in tensions and strained relationships. Finally, an improvement may occur, as some adjustive technique is successful.

Family organization then becomes stabilized at a new level. At each phase of the crisis there is a reshuffling of roles among family members, changes in status and prestige, changes in "self" and "other" images, shifts in family solidarity and self-sufficiency and in visibility of the crisis to outsiders. While the crisis is in progress, considerable mental conflict is engendered in all family members and personality distortion occurs. The phases vary in length and intensity, depending on the nature of the crisis and the nature of the individual involved in it.

When one of the adults in a family becomes an alcoholic, there are usually recurrent, subsidiary crises that complicate the overall situation and attempts at resolving it. Shame, unemployment, impoverishment, desertion and return, non-support, infidelity, violence, imprisonment, illness and progressive dissension may also occur. For most types of family crisis there are cultured prescriptions for what to do to end the crisis. In the case of alcoholism, however, despite some lessening of the social stigma, our culture still takes the position that this problem is shameful and should not occur. Thus, when facing alcoholism, the family is in a social situation that is largely unstructured, so it must find the techniques for handling the crisis through trial and error and without social support. In many respects there are marked similarities between the type of family crisis brought about by alcoholism and those precipitated by mental illness.

Full-blown alcoholism is rarely a sudden event. It is usually heralded by widely spaced incidents of excessive drinking, each of which sets off a small family crisis. Both husband and wife try to find reasons for the episode, hoping to avoid the family situations that appear to have caused the drinking. In their search for explanations they may try to define the situation as controllable, understandable and "perfectly normal." Between drinking episodes both may feel guilty about their behavior and about their impact on each other. Gradually, not only the drinking problem but also other problems in the marriage are denied or side stepped.

It takes time before the non-alcoholic spouse realizes that the drinking is neither normal nor controllable behavior. It takes the alcoholic considerably longer to come to the same conclusion. The cultural view that alcoholics are skid row bums and/or are constantly inebriated also serves to keep the situation clouded. Friends compound the confusion. If the spouse compares his or her situation with them, some show parallels in behavior and others are in marked contrast. If the spouse consults friends, they tend to discount his or her concerns, making it easier to deny that a problem exists and adding to mounting guilt.

During this stage, social isolation of the family often begins. To a certain degree, others withdraw after one or more episodes of inappropriate behavior by the alcoholic. For the most part, however, the family withdrawing itself socially brings about the isolation. Members fear the reaction of others to the increasingly unpredictable public behavior of the alcoholic; they fear that their own inability to cope effectively with such episodes will be obvious to outsiders; they fear others will come to know the full extent of the drinking. To protect themselves from their distress and from what they see as inevitable social exclusion, the family cuts down on social activities and withdraws into the home.

The next stage begins when the family defines the alcoholic's drinking behavior as "not normal". Frantic efforts are now made to eliminate the problem. Lacking clear-cut cultural prescriptions for a solution to this situation, such effects must be trial-and-error in nature. In rapid succession, the wife threatens to leave the husband, babies him during his hangovers, drinks with him, hides or empties his bottles, curtails money, tries to understand his problem, keeps liquor handy for him and nags at him. Similar sequences of events occur when a husband attempts to deal with an alcoholic wife. In any case, efforts to change the situation fail. Gradually the family becomes so preoccupied with the problem of discovering how to keep the alcoholic sober that long-term goals recede into the background.

At this time, isolation for the family reaches its peak. This isolation magnifies the importance of all intra-family interactions and events. Almost all thought becomes drink-centered. Drinking comes to symbolize all conflicts between husband and wife, and even parent-child conflicts are regarded as indirect derivatives of the drinking behavior. Attempts increase to keep the social visibility of the drinking at the lowest possible level.

The husband-wife alienation also accelerates. Each feels resentful of the other. Each feels misunderstood and unable to understand. Both search frantically for the reasons for the drinking, believing that if the reason could be discovered, all family members could gear their behavior in a way to make the drinking unnecessary.

The wife feels increasingly inadequate as a wife, mother, woman and person. She may feel she has failed to make a happy and united home for her husband and children. The husband's frequent comments to the effect that "her" behavior causes his drinking, and her own concern that this may be true, intensifies the process of self-devaluation. The non-alcoholic husband also feels inadequate as a marital partner, frequently feeling lonely and abandoned by his spouse. He may experience great concern about the deterioration of the household and increasing anxiety as to the effects of his wife's alcoholism on their children. He, too, is plagued by feelings of guilt and helplessness. A fitting title for this stage could be, "What's the use?" Nothing seems effective in stabilizing the alcoholic. Efforts to change the situation become, at best, sporadic. Behavior is geared to relieve tensions rather than to achieve goals. The family gives up trying to understand the alcoholic. They do not care if the neighbors know about the drinking. The children may be told that their mother or father is a drunk. They are no longer required to show that parent affection or respect. When the alcoholic parent is male, the myth that the father still has an important status in the family is dropped when he no longer supports them, is imprisoned, is caught in infidelity, or disappears for long periods of time. The family ceases to care about its self-sufficiency and may begin to resort to public agencies for financial and other help, often feeling a loss of self-respect as a result.

The non-alcoholic partner becomes concerned about his or her sanity. Such individuals find themselves engaging in tension-relieving behavior that is clearly goalless. They are aware of feeling tense, anxious and hostile. They come to think of the pre-crisis self as "the real me" and become frightened at how much they have changed.

The disorganized state usually ends when some alcoholic-related crisis, which may be serious or may simply represent the straw that broke the camel's back, forces the family to take organized action.

In some families this action takes the form of a physical separation from the alcoholic. In others, where such a step is felt to be too extreme, there is an effort to restructure the family along new lines of authority. When reorganization is thus attempted, this new phase has as its distinguishing characteristic the spouse who takes over. The alcoholic is ignored or is assigned the status of a recalcitrant child. When the non-drinking spouse's obligations to the alcoholic conflict with those toward the children, the decisions favor the children. Family ranks are closed progressively and the drinker is excluded.

As a result of the changed family organization, the alcoholic behavior constitutes less of a problem. Hostility diminishes, as the family no longer expects a change. Feelings of pity, exasperation and protectiveness may arise.

This reorganization has a stabilizing effect on the children. They find their environment and their non-alcoholic parent more consistent. Their relationships are more clearly defined. Guilt and anxiety diminish as they come to accept the non-drinker's view that the cause of the problem drinking is not connected with the behavior of family members.

Long-term family goals and planning may begin again. If she has not done so already, the wife may take a job. If she does, she alleviates several problems. The family manages financially without the alcoholic; the wife becomes less socially isolated and is able to regain a sense of competence. If necessary, help from public agencies is accepted and no longer impairs family self-respect. By taking over, the wife gradually regains her sense of worth. Her concerns about her emotional health decrease.

The husband of an alcoholic wife may start to cope with household and family problems by making arrangements for childcare, by hiring household help, by increasingly taking part in activities with his children outside the home.

Despite such stabilization, however, subsidiary crises multiply. The alcoholic is violent or withdraws more often. Unemployment, legal problems and hospitalization occur more frequently. Each crisis is temporarily disruptive to the new family organization. The recognition of these events as being caused by alcoholism, however, prevents a complete family breakdown.

The most serious type of crisis occurs if the alcoholic recognizes that he or she has a drinking problem and makes an effort to get help. Hope is mobilized. The family attempts to open ranks in order to give the alcoholic the maximum change for recovery. Roles are partially reshuffled and attempts are made at attitude change, only to be disrupted again if treatment is unsuccessful.

Many husbands and some wives find it necessary to leave their alcoholic spouse outright. The problems involved in separating from the alcoholic are similar to problems involved in separation for other reasons. Some, however, are more difficult. The wife who could count on some financial support from her husband in earlier stages of alcoholism can no longer be sure of such assistance.

The husband finds himself without emotional support. The mental conflict about deserting a sick person must be resolved, as well as painful feelings of responsibility for the alcoholism. The family that has experienced violence from the alcoholic may fear that separation will intensify the violence. When the decision is made to live apart because of the drinking, the alcoholic often gives up drinking for a while, thereby removing, at least temporarily, what is apparently the major reason for separation and creating, in the process, much confusion and guilt in the non-alcoholic partner.

Other events, however, may have made separation more acceptable. The non-alcoholic spouse may have learned that the family can run smoothly without the alcoholic; taking over control bolsters the spouse's self-confidence. The family's orientation has shifted from inaction to action.

When recovery is actually underway, the family enters a difficult period of adjustment and reorganization. After many years of living in an alcoholic situation, a husband and wife now beginning a sober marriage may find their expectation of each other to be unrealistic and idealistic. Many problems arise if either spouse has managed the family alone for a considerable time. When the alcoholic wishes to be reinstated as a parent or as a full marital partner, difficulties inevitably follow. For example, children are often unable to accept the alcoholic's resumption of the parental role.

Often the alcoholic parent tries to manage this change overnight and the very pressure put on children leads to defeat.

The spouse has difficulty believing that the change is permanent and is often unwilling to relinquish control of family affairs, even though this may be necessary to another's sobriety. Past failures to handle responsibility were a disaster for the family.

Accustomed to avoiding issues that might upset the alcoholic, the spouse has difficulty discussing problems openly. If managing roles are resumed, the spouse often feels resentful of the alcoholic's intrusion into territory once regarded as one's own. If detrimental decisions are made, the former feeling of superiority may be activated and may affect the relationship.

Gradually, the difficulties related to alcoholism recede into the past and family adjustment at some level is achieved. Problems about drinking may show

up occasionally, perhaps when the time comes for a decision about permitting the children to drink or when there are social pressures to drink.

The major goal of the families of most alcoholics is to find some way of bringing about a change in the drinking. Often this means getting the alcoholic into a treatment program. It is not at all unusual for family members to have mixed feelings toward the treatment agency. Hope that the alcoholic may recover is rekindled and, if sobriety ensues for any length of time, they are grateful. At the same time they often feel resentment that an outside agency can accomplish what they have tried to do for years. They also resent the emotional support the alcoholic receives from the treatment agency, while they are left to cope with still another change in their relationship to him or her without such emotional support.

It is fortunate that in recent years most treatment programs for alcoholics have come to see the importance of involving family members.

Most often it is the spouse who is included in the alcoholic's treatment but sometimes children are also asked to take part. Joint treatment aims at getting a better understanding of the underlying emotional disturbances, the relationship between the alcoholic and the people who most frequently interact with the drinking behavior, and the treatment process. Joint therapy of the alcoholic and his/her family also has other advantages. Joint therapy emphasizes the marriage. With both partners coming for help, there is less likelihood that undertaking treatment will be construed as an admission of guilt or one against the other will use that therapy as a weapon. The non-alcoholic's entrance into therapy is an unspoken admission that that person also needs to change. It represents a hopeful attitude on the part of the alcoholic and the partner that recovery is possible, which helps them work things out together as a family unit.

A very important resource for the families of alcoholics is the Al-Anon Family Group program. While Al-Anon is similar in many important ways to other programs, which help or include the families of alcoholics, it has some very significant differences. Unlike most programs, Al-Anon does not require that the alcoholic be undergoing treatment. It helps the families of recovering alcoholics but also the families of those alcoholics who are still not making any efforts to become sober. It helps members of the immediate family of alcoholics but it also opens its doors to *all* family members, parents, siblings and more distant relatives.

The members of an Al-Anon group with which this author is familiar receive from one another understanding of their problems and feelings, as well as emotional support that facilitates changes of attitude and behavior. They are given basic information about solutions to common problems, about the treatment process and about the nature of the illness of alcoholism. Shame is alleviated and hope engendered. The non-alcoholic spouses gain perspective on what has happened to their families and on the possibilities of change toward greater stability. Anxiety diminishes in an almost visible fashion. As they gain perspective on the situation, behavior tends to become more realistic and rewarding. By no means the least important effects derived from membership in recovery groups are structuring and feelings of security this engendered.

Recovery has a very special part to play in the organization of those families whose alcoholic members achieve sobriety through the A.A. program. Through participation in Al-Anon's program, family members are able to have a recovering and growing experience parallel to that of the alcoholic. They, too, are surrounded by warmth, understanding, concern and support while they are recovering. In a very meaningful sense there is a sharing of recovery that helps each individual family member to find himself and the family as a whole, to reorganize in a new and shared philosophy: a way of life without alcohol.

Physicians, nurses, social workers, counselors and other health care professionals have found the Al-Anon Fellowship to be an invisible ally. Referral to Al-Anon can provide the distressed alcoholic family members with many unique benefits.

Most people in our society are poorly educated about alcoholism. Many still consider the alcoholic to be "weak-willed" and family members of alcoholics are no exception.

Family members benefit enormously from learning that alcoholism is a disease. Identifying the "family problem" helps prevent what otherwise can be an unpredictable series of worsening crises. The family learns to cope both intellectually and emotionally. Understanding the alcoholic blackout throws light on what otherwise may appear to be a totally inexplicable situation...or even outright lying. Understanding the "loss of controls" phenomenon can explain the apparent "weak will".

While Al-Anon is not merely an educational tool, Al-Anon meetings and literature do provide an excellent source of information about this complex illness. Those who have lived with the problem of alcoholism have much to share about it.

Not infrequently, some individuals attending the meetings will learn enough about the disease to identify themselves as alcoholics. The subsequent steps toward involvement with Alcoholics Anonymous are much easier to take with an Al-Anon background.

Alcoholism is still a stigmatized disease. While this makes it more difficult for the alcoholic to accept the illness, it also makes it more difficult for the family to accept that alcoholism exists within it. The stigma prevents both the alcoholic and the family members from going for help, so that the associated shame and guilt will also be major roadblocks in successfully referring a prospective new Al-

Anon member to the fellowship. However, if the family learns about alcoholism, begins to accept it as a disease and sees that others can talk openly at support meetings, the stigma slowly dissipates.

Denial of the illness is a major defense for both the alcoholic and the family members. Some aspects of the denial system are based simply on lack of education. Others are bolstered by the stigma of the disease. Al-Anon can provide the family of the alcoholic not only with assistance in both of these aspects, as described above, but also with more subtle consideration of this complex psychological defense mechanism.

Newcomers hear others speak at meetings and can relate to common experiences and feelings. Denial that they have been adversely affected by alcoholism, denial of the roles they have played in the maladaptive family system, denial of the support they have given that inadvertently enabled the alcoholism to progress, can all break down. The supportive and accepting atmosphere at most Al-Anon meetings is conducive to the relaxation of defense mechanisms.

Al-Anon is probably best described as "The Fellowship." Many family members come to their first meeting believing they are the only ones who have lived through the private type of hell that living with an alcoholic can be. The friendly faces and warm greetings may be all that nervous newcomers need to

keep them coming back. As members who have been suffering in isolation find the ability to relate and share on a feeling level, close friendships grow and develop.

Although, to the scientifically trained health care professional, Al-Anon may at first appear superficially simplistic, or perhaps religious in nature, it is in fact a rich and complex positive-thinking, self-help program that has withstood the test of time and has proven to be ingeniously designed to assist family members into a more satisfying life.

A support group meeting is an experience difficult to describe and is best understood through exposure. I would strongly recommend that any health care professional attend an "open" meeting. If the professional has a family connection with alcoholism, any meeting can be attended. In addition to providing a valuable professional experience it is likely to offer valuable personal experience as well. If the professional does not qualify as being a friend or family member of an alcoholic and is thus not eligible for membership, I suggest they phone the local Al-Anon answering service, identify themselves as an interested professional and obtain information on attending an "open" Al-Anon meeting, where members welcome any interested person.

Al-Anon groups are extremely diverse, comprising all socioeconomic levels. Professionally speaking, my initial primary consideration in referring family members to Al-Anon are to find a member or group with whom they might most easily identify and relate. This might mean referral to specially named Al-Anon groups, which, while open to all, may be comprised primarily of men, physicians, homosexuals or adult children of alcoholics. Such specially targeted referrals may, in many instances, increase the chances that the newcomer will form a lasting attachment to recovery. However, the inexperienced health care professional should anticipate a less than enthusiastic response when recommending Al-Anon for the family members of an alcoholic. In my experience, referral to Al-Anon is just as difficult as referral to Alcoholics Anonymous. (The most difficult referral in my experience is to Alateen…especially if neither parent is in Al-Anon or Alcoholics Anonymous.) The health care professional in whom the family members have confidence is in an excellent position to make a referral. If the professional is knowledgeable about Al-Anon and especially if the professional has been to an Al-Anon meeting and has read some Al-Anon literature, the referral recommendation is even more likely to be acted upon.

Anyone whose life is or has been adversely affected by a relationship to an alcoholic can benefit from a Twelve Step way of life. This certainly includes all first-degree relatives (children, spouses, siblings and parents) of alcoholics but may also include second-degree relatives (if a close or "live-together" relationship exists or has existed) lovers, fiancees or close friends of alcoholics.

The professional's primary difficulty may be in identifying these individuals among their patients or clients. It is unusual for family members to present themselves for help and volunteer the information that their problem is related to the stress of an alcoholic family system. It often happens that distressed family members are not aware of the source of their discomfort. Even if the family member is aware, the professional may have to probe carefully for the information.

Family members of alcoholics present physicians and nurses with an endless variety of stress-related problems: gastrointestinal complaints, low-back pain, headaches, insomnia, anxiety, depression etc. Social Workers and Counselors see the stress of the alcoholic family system in adults as deteriorating work performance, marital separation or divorce, physical and sexual abuse.

Children may exhibit school or behavioral problems, hyperactivity, runaway episodes, juvenile delinquency and a variety of psychological difficulties. Key symptoms also include being out of touch with feelings and having difficulty with trust. Indeed, the manifestations of the suffering alcoholic family members are almost endless.

In questioning any patient, it is reasonable to inquire about possible family stress. If the response is positive, the professional…remembering that alcoholism is the leading cause of family stress…may then inquire more directly

about "drinking problems" or drinking behavior that bothers one, rather than alcoholism per say. In my experience, the distressed family member does not usually know what alcoholism is.

In attempting to obtain information about possible drinking problems in the family, the professional must keep in mind that alcoholism is typically treated as the "family secret". The patient/client will probably have to develop a sense of trust in the helping professional before disclosing information never before shared with anyone outside the family. It will be especially difficult to learn about physical violence, neglect and incestuous behavior.

There has been tremendous growth in the professional recognition of problems resulting from the alcoholic family system. The health care professional astute enough to recognize individuals in distress as a result of their alcoholic family experience is in a unique position to refer them to other sources of help. Al-Anon should be the professional's primary resource. (2)

What is meant by good mental health? The experts use expressions like "feeling confident and comfortable about oneself", "being interested in others and considerate" and "able to meet the demands of life." In talking about family life, words like "supportive", "cooperative", "flexible", "tolerant" and "dependable" describe the ideals to strive for. Of course, people fall short of these ideals in their personal lives and in their families, but some achieve them now and then, at

least in part. For many living with the problem of alcoholism these moments of personal satisfaction in a pleasant family life are infrequent and tentative. There is little consistent joy in life…sometimes none at all.

From the viewpoint of the mental health professional that works with alcoholic families, the Twelve Step way of life is a blessing because it provides a model program, freely available almost everywhere, which addresses the emotional needs of these troubled people with accuracy, simplicity and thoroughness.

Al-Anon offers something a therapist cannot provide: the social support and comfort of fellowship with others who understand alcoholism in its many manifestations. Sharing experiences with others and taking hope from them offers relief from the anguish, self-doubt, bitterness, hurt and the fears that often torment alcoholic families. When these people meet together, they experience the "shared honesty of mutual vulnerability openly acknowledged." The frequent repetition of the experience at A.A. and Al-Anon meetings, coupled with efforts to live at home according to the Twelve Step program, is reassuring and healing to troubled spirits in a way that defies explanation. They regain the ability to reflect on their lives…not only on their problems, but also on solutions.

Once the fellowship has begun to give people hope and a renewal of faith, Al-Anon members make a dramatic change in their perception of alcoholism. (Instead of focusing on the person who most obviously needs help, Al-Anon urges family members to examine themselves: how have they unwittingly become their own worst enemies (and the alcoholic's, too) as they have struggled to help someone else? This process of self-examination is easy for some: the Al-Anon message is like a light turning on. It is a long, slow process for most family members, however, to learn how their anxieties, anger, resentments and preoccupation with someone else's problem have aggravated and maintained it rather than solving it. Throughout this process they must be constantly reminded through the Al-Anon Fellowship that they have always done the best they could do at the time. Families need to be reminded that almost anyone would have done many of the same things; given the situation they were in. Helping people to pull themselves out of these situations is the mission of Al-Anon, and this is done without recrimination toward the alcoholic, or toward the family or toward the past. To quit blaming is essential.

Once family members have relearned how to reflect on what is happening in their lives, once they can be both realistic and optimistic at the same time and once they have begun to see with some accuracy how they themselves have become involved in the problem of alcoholism, Al-Anon encourages its members to follow the Twelve Step guidelines that help them to be less anxious and more thoughtful as they go about their daily lives. Who could ask more from a program for restoring good mental health?

But Al-Anon is much more than a good mental health program. The fellowship, together with the universal principles for right living that it espouses, can lead people to a renewed appreciation of life. Living life fully and joyfully is the goal of the Twelve Step way of life. One key element in taking a new approach to life is the basic concept of detachment with love.

This is ground where the professional must tread lightly and where the fellowship of Al-Anon can move more confidently. Al-Anon urges its members to understand that they are powerless to change another person. This is a very hard thing to realize fully, especially when that person is in big trouble and everyone knows it. That they love an alcoholic…even enough to leave, if that has to be…but that they cannot make the alcoholic be different, is a terrible truth and a wonderful one at the same time.

Paradoxically, detachment with love helps people discover their own spiritual lives as they realize that they too are in the hands of a Higher Power. The spirit of fellowship is essential to a process of learning; understanding can be seen in the faces of recovering members.

Detachment helps people to know a higher form of love than they may have known when they were preoccupied with the alcoholic…always trying to second-guess the next move, the next disaster. Trying to keep the alcoholic out of trouble, cheering him up, encouraging him to pull himself together…all these are loving things to do. But is it not a greater love to help only when it is truly helpful; and, finally to allow the alcoholic to know the consequences of his or her own behavior? Al-Anon thinks so. How is it possible to draw the line between the things to be done to make the situation better and the things that cannot be done? Al-Anon urges its members to ponder this question in their hearts.

Love turns into desperation when people are unable to recognize the point at which, in helping others, they have taken too much upon themselves. Al-Anon asks its members to stop obsessively devising new strategies for dealing with the alcoholic. Instead, members are reminded at every meeting and in the Serenity Prayer, to consider the difference between the things they can and cannot do in helping others…especially those they love most.

As this essential difference is defined, family members begin to feel more confident about themselves and, therefore, more patient with their loved ones, more tolerant of them. They become better able to make good decisions about their own lives.

Great progress has been made by professionals during the past 15 to 20 years in expanding the treatment of alcoholism to include the family. Yet the difficulty in admitting the existence of the problem…the outstanding symptom of the family illness…still prevents many people from seeking treatment. Until recently the major focus was on alcoholics, with mini-programs added for their families. In the past few years many professionals have recognized the need for treatment that addresses the family's systems; primary programs for families are being provided now in many places.

Al-Anon Family Groups, which include Alateen, have been helping families of alcoholics since the 1940's, providing the most direct and continuous help for families and friends of alcoholics. The term "family member" is used here to imply anyone whose personal life has been negatively affected by another's drinking; this includes relatives, colleagues and friends. With statistics indicating that approximately 40 to 50 million Americans are affected by alcoholism, it would seem that Al-Anon should be 4 or 5 times as large as Alcoholics Anonymous. Instead, the membership is only about two-fifths the size. It is obvious that, despite advances in professional services, many family members are not being reached at all.

Much has been accomplished in helping alcoholics toward recovery in the last 20 years. The success rate has been raised by early intervention, motivation into treatment and continuous follow up. It has been proven that alcoholics do not have to "hit bottom" to get well but rather, need to be in a situation where treatment is accessible.

These same concepts are equally important to the treatment of families. For, wherever families remain uninvolved in their recovery program, the seeds of the illness continue to be passed on to the next generation. Every professional alcoholism program should have as its objective introducing the family members to Al-Anon and helping them to avail themselves of its support.

Families need to learn of the illness in a gentle, easy to accept, yet forthright manner; they need to identify their own experience with the illness and accept their own need for a recovery plan. Al-Anon should be the main aftercare resource for families, as Alcoholics Anonymous is for the alcoholic.

For family members, alcoholism causes a progressive inability to predict their own behavior because of the growing preoccupation with and reaction to another person's drinking. Generally speaking, if a person is wondering whether alcoholism is a problem, it probably is. Family members need to hear that the emotions they feel are a normal reaction to alcoholism. Frequently, that experience is a free-floating but pervasive fear. They are afraid of the alcoholic's reactions and are prepared to settle for "peace at any price." They worry about bills, accidents and job losses (the alcoholic's and, in some cases, their own.) As they attempt to deal with the erratic, irrational behavior of the drinker, they become confused and increasingly guilty and preoccupied. As their lives become compulsively centered on trying to get the alcoholic to stop drinking through unsuccessful efforts to manipulate and control, most of their actions only enable the alcoholic to continue the drinking. Family members are caught in a cycle of repetitive non-helpful behavior that leaves them frustrated, angry and alone. They feel helpless and hopeless.

Manifesting these feelings, attitudes and actions, together with a lack of understanding of the disease, families foster the hope that if the alcoholic would stop drinking, everything would be different and all right. Families feel that it is not their lives, but the alcoholic's life, that is out of control.

The role of the professional is to help family members break through their own denial and motivate them into a recovery process. They can ask families a few simple questions:

Has your life been disrupted by someone else's drinking?

Are you preoccupied with the drinking?

Have you begun to dislike some of the things you say and do? (3)

Any "yes" answer immediately helps them to identify how the disease of alcoholism has affected them.

The next requirement is for family members to learn that their recovery does not depend on the alcoholic's. They must accept alcoholism as an illness and understand that the alcoholic cannot drink in moderation. This enables them to separate their own lives from the alcoholic's and to allow the drinker to be responsible for his or her own actions. Regardless of the current circumstances, family members learn that they can become capable of making wise decisions and taking constructive action while being responsive to others. They can grow to have serenity and satisfaction with their lives and their relationships.

In the early stages of recovery, family members learn about detachment and become willing to separate their emotional lives from the alcoholic's. Often newcomers to Al-Anon feel that detachment looks like coldness or indifference. Some even think it means to separate physically from the alcoholic. Professionals can assist newcomers to understand the practical necessity of letting go, only to move back enough so they do not interfere with the natural consequences of the drinking behavior and the need for the alcoholic to rebuild his or her own life. Family members must free themselves from the compulsion to "fix" things. The following exercise can demonstrate detachment in a small way:

Stand in front of a full-length mirror. Get as close as you can.

Notice how limited your vision and perspective are. All you

can see are your own two eyes staring back at you. Notice
further how this limits your ability to concentrate on other
things. Now step back just a little; you can see your whole
self. Your vision, perspective and ability to think have all
expanded considerably. (4)

For Al-Anon members, detachment is the culmination of applying
themselves to all the steps and slogans of the Al-Anon program, especially
the first step. This necessitates accepting a concept of powerlessness over
another human being and over alcoholism. In order to reach the kind of
detachment that Al-Anon members strive for, the individual must come to
understand and accept his or her own feelings, attitudes, prejudices and
actions and be committed to changing them in a healthy way.

It is obvious that issues of recovery for family members are difficult and
complex. Although the outlook for recovery for families has improved
considerably over the past 10 or 12 years, many families are still left
unmotivated and uninnovated. Professionals, whose help may be needed
for initial treatment and during some phases of recovery, should carefully
refer families to Al-Anon and support their continued active membership.
Al-Anon members, on the other hand, need to be alert and receptive to
the cooperation with professionals, which eases the integration of family
members into the fellowship. Willing and knowledgeable cooperation on
the part of each group will do much to insure that all persons affected by
this serious, chronic illness have the opportunity to recover.

One of the most wonderful aspects of recovery is the capacity of the
suggested Twelve Steps to provide guidelines for a progressively healthier
and fuller life. We hear so much about the effectiveness of Twelve Step
work in helping those affected by a drinking alcoholic achieve the

detachment needed to deal with that painful situation that we sometimes forget the rewards the program continues to offer in long-term living. It has been said often that Alcoholics Anonymous is not only about
drinking: it is also very much about living.

The concept of detachment provides a good example. Often professionals have difficulty understanding the true nature of detachment. It
does not indicate a chasm between the Al-Anon member and the alcoholic, nor does detachment intend to convey a life of isolation from the
problem drinker. Rather, detachment provides a platform for the practice
of a more appropriate responsibility for oneself and others. It is in such
way that we see how the Al-Anon program is beautifully crafted to provide
a proven method of approaching life.

Many of us, both Al-Anon members and professionals, are likely to feel
that dealing with an alcoholic's wife, husband, child, parent, lover, co-
worker or friend is dictated by that person's behavior rather than by any
needs, problem or circumstances of the Al-Anon member. If we do not
recognize that both parties to a relationship have a responsibility, then we
preclude the use of the Al-Anon program in its fullest applicability. Most
professionals who work with families of alcoholics understand the way in
which the program meets the present concerns and prepares for the future
needs of each individual in dealing with various living situations, particularly with relationships.

People who have lived for any length of time in a close relationship
with an alcoholic have found themselves engaged to some extent in trying
to control outcomes, especially with regard to the alcoholic's drinking. It is
a major adjustment to understand that one can only be responsible for
one's own behavior and must therefore let go of a need to control the
result…part of which invalidates another person's behavior. Having

achieved such a major shift in perception and motivation in one area, it seems reasonable to recognize the value of practicing this principle in all one's affairs.

Many family members reach out for help, either to a professional agency or to Al-Anon, before the alcoholic in their lives has been able to accept any help for his or her problem. One of the first things any knowledgeable resource will help the concerned person understand is the need to focus on oneself rather than on the behavior of the alcoholic. Many families are in the throes of pain and confusion as they reel from one crisis to the next, feeling inextricably controlled by all the trouble and sadness that the alcoholic accumulates. They begin to feel that they have very little to say about how their own life works out. Detachment is a valuable concept and tool for these people in disentangling their thinking and their reactions from the behavior of the drinker. However, the very strength of this mechanism contains some potential drawbacks. Many of us have seen, and sometimes have continued to focus on, the great value for the Al-Anon member in detachment from the alcoholic. A genuine sense of detachment can be the source of so much relief and so much change in a brief period of time that it is seen as nothing short of miraculous. What we must understand, and help the newcomer to the program understand, is that detachment is not isolation. Detachment is not a wall; it is a bridge across which the Al-Anon member may begin a new approach to life and relationships in general.

As we go through life, most of us engage, to some degree, in manipulation of those around us. Similarly many of us feel a certain amount of control being exercised by others in determining the course and quality of our lives. In an alcoholic family, it is not unusual to see all the family members, including the alcoholic, veering from a highly manipulative to a highly victimized mentality. We sometimes see great amounts of energy invested in determining the truth of these changes and counter-changes of exploitation/victimization within the family. In many instances it may be much less important to determine the truth of these perceptions than it is to change the dynamics that gave rise to them…in other words, the cultivation of healthy attitudes and appropriate detachment in shaping one's own thoughts and behavior.

When the active alcoholism has been dealt with either through the sobriety of the alcoholic or through his or her removal from the immediate family environment, it becomes increasingly important to recognize the need to utilize the Al-Anon program as a guide in all one's relationships. To continue the focus on dealing with the sober and/or absent alcoholic largely or exclusively is to limit rather severely the potential for recovery of the Al-Anon member. To move our earlier parallel one step along in the recovery continuum, just as Alcoholics Anonymous is about living more than it is about drinking, so Al-Anon is about living more than it is about dealing with a non-drinking alcoholic. I believe that, until we can shift our focus from the interaction with the alcoholic to a broader view of our self-responsibility in approaching life, we are still in the active throes of the family illness of alcoholism.

It is much easier to characterize a relapse for an alcoholic than it is for a member of Al-Anon, but this does not mean that the phenomenon is any less real or frequent, nor is it any less recognizable to the seasoned observer than is the drinking behavior of the relapsed alcoholic. There are signals and symptoms apparent to the veteran Al-Anon member, as well as to the experienced professional, which indicate the need for a non-alcoholic to modify his or her thoughts and behavior if recovery is to continue as a progressively enhanced life. These indicators usually take the form of reverting to old habits in familiar situations and relationships. They can just as readily appear, however, in new situations and relationships if a person is not on guard. Again, true detachment is a wonderful resource to keep one's balance between responsibility for self and responsibility to and for others. There are many occasions when we all engage in enabling destructive or inappropriate behavior in other people. This can happen in the family, in the workplace, in social settings, or anywhere else where people interact with one another. It can be done in ignorance, out of a mistaken notion of kindness or concern, or because it is easier and less threatening to the enabler. All, Al-Anon member, professional and us alike, have seen this in people around us and perhaps have discovered it in our own behavior. The danger lies not so much in what we are "causing" or "preventing" but in the resurgence of the mental attitude that we are responsible for someone's behavior and consequently for the results of that behavior. Most instances are not so obvious or dramatic as that enabling that may have gone on with the alcoholic. Nonetheless, we still need to be conscious of the potential for this unhealthy and unproductive behavior and to guard against it.

There is yet another area where I believe detachment has a central role. That is in the relationship of an Al-Anon member with a Higher Power, as each individual defines that power. Again, an appropriate level of responsibility...humility, if you will...is essential for the healthiest and most fruitful direction of spiritual growth. Probably nowhere is this dealt with more clearly and more succinctly than in the Serenity Prayer: "God grant me the serenity to accept the things I cannot change, courage to change the things I can, and the wisdom to know the difference."

With one's Higher Power, it is also essential to understand the need for responsible behavior and the acceptance of the outcomes that proceed from it. Even in this special relationship, there is often an inclination to try to manipulate the results. The Al-Anon member has come to recognize that he or she cannot control the drinking of the alcoholic. Yet many are still unable to see that prayers couched in terms of specific requests and specific results may often be just as self-defeating and just as unhealthy as is trying to control another's behavior by reactions and plans. Most people in Al-Anon come to understand the futility of attempting to control another person's behavior through their own behavior. They understand the need to focus on themselves, on the way they are thinking and acting, rather than attempting to control and dictate to the other person. How much more obvious the thought should be (and yet how seldom it is!) that one cannot control one's Higher Power. In using the slogan "Let Go and Let God," how often is added a silent tagline, "but Let God do it *this* way." There is often a failure to recognize the resurgence of an old pattern of destructive behavior in what most of us see as a positive reliance on the spiritual relationship.

Similarly, while many Al-Anon members recognize the value of detachment in dealing with family members, friends, business associates and others, they may shy away from the application of detachment in their relationship with their own spirituality and the embodiment of that in a Higher Power.

I believe that, as an Al-Anon member pursues and grows in the practice of recommended Twelve Step program of recovery, the Serenity Prayer comes to embody the only request, which needs to be made of that Higher Power. If one can concentrate on a responsible approach to the journey of life, the Higher Power will take responsibility for the destination. To have such an attitude is the ultimate gift of Al-Anon, not only to its members, but also to all of us who are able to embrace this simple, powerful, universal program. (5)

The concept of the "Adult Child" is spreading rapidly and is used to refer to the great number of adults who were parented in a home affected by alcoholism. Unlike people not raised in alcoholic homes, these are adults who characteristically experience greater difficulty in their ability to trust, to identify and express feelings and to ask for what they need. They experience greater difficulty in intimate relationships and are more likely to experience depression. The term "Adult Child" legitimizes the experiences of such a person during childhood and encapsulates a description of his or her problem as an adult. As is true for the alcoholic and the spouse, the Adult Child is in need of direct therapeutic intervention and the opportunity to enter a recovery process. (6)

The self-help groups of Alcoholics Anonymous and Al-Anon are often found to be the greatest resources to the recovery of the alcoholic and spouse. They not only stop the active addiction process, they offer an ongoing recovery process that becomes a very satisfying lifestyle to those who follow their Twelve Steps and Traditions. With this endorsement, it has been most natural to assist Adult Child clients to see Al-Anon as a viable resource for them. What is particularly beneficial about Al-Anon as a viable resource for them? What is particularly beneficial about Al-Anon as a viable resource is that it addresses and ultimately affects the basic issues of 1) not talking; 2) not feeling; 3) not trusting; 4) guilt; 5) control; and 6) isolation.

Most young children in alcoholic families learn that it is not safe to talk honestly and openly about what is happening in their lives. This stems from a variety of reasons; shame; loyalty; uncertainty about what to say; lack of models or permission from others to talk; and fear of reprimand and negative consequences when they do speak. The support group of Al-Anon provides Adult Children with an arena where they are not ashamed to speak. Al-Anon is an environment in which Adult Children do not feel they are betraying themselves. They are given the opportunity and support to share as they choose, discovering that there are no reprimands for being honest.

Adult Children usually demonstrate a great fear of feelings. They find that, through the group experience, their fears are usually put in proper perspective. In Al-Anon, people share sadness, embarrassment, anger, and fear, in the process coming to realize that they don't "fall apart". Recovery provides models for sharing honestly, as well as validation for the feelings when expressed. Group participants are not criticized for sharing their pain. Instead, they receive understanding and empathy.

Further, recovery offers Adult Children many dynamics that assist them in becoming more trusting. Recovery groups are a psychologically safe place; there is acceptance and unconditional love from the start, a bonding based on the common identities. *Trust Takes Time, But Does Occur!*

Adult Children meetings are a setting in which "ACOA's" learn that they are not responsible for things they have no control over, which lessens their guilt. They are repeatedly told, "You are not responsible." In addition, these meetings provide feedback allowing the Adult Child to set appropriate limits in order to help themselves and not enable others. In the process, the Adult Child begins to find self-esteem.

Control is a major issue for Adult Children, in that they have a strong need either to be in total control or to feel no control over any aspect of their lives. The First Step of Twelve Step recovery immediately says, "I am powerless." For some Adult Children, acceptance of powerlessness means they do not have all the answers. Many Adult Children readily accept this and are relieved to be confirmed in their perceived helplessness. At the same time, they are also able to get appropriate feedback as to the power they do have in their lives. For other Adult Children, such acceptance marks the beginning of an awareness that they can no longer do it all by themselves.

The concept of acknowledging powerlessness accompanied by the concept of "surrender" means to let go of control, which for every Adult Child is very frightening. Control has meant survival for the Adult Child. Adult

Children fight this because they have taken such pride in their ability to manage, achieve and perform. Although in this sense frightening, recovery offers Adult Children a realistic perspective of their own power and helps to ease rigidity in their need to be in control.

In treating the Adult Child, Twelve Step recovery is typically indicated as a viable source for help. Nonetheless, many have gone to Twelve Step meetings and, for various reasons, have chosen not to return. This reluctance needs to be addressed. Others are simply unaware that recovery exists; many have misconceptions recognizing that not all Adult Children will choose to use a "program." It is wise to insist they see it as an option before they reject it.

It is important to ask about a client's knowledge and experience with Al-Anon, but sometimes attendance at meetings is not suggested until a more trusting relationship is developed. Recovery may be presented as a resource the client will find helpful. If clients demonstrate any interest in recovery, they can be offered a directory and particular meetings might be suggested. If a client expresses misconceptions and negative biases toward a program, recovery might be proposed at another time when the client may be better able to see this as a possible option.

New clients are typically scared, non-trusting and confused people. It has often taken all their strength to come to a counselor's office. If clients are referred to another resource of any kind too quickly, this is often perceived to work with them so they are less frightened, have more clarity about what it is they are experiencing and are able to develop a greater sense of trust. Once they know that they can rely upon a counselor, they know that they will not be "abandoned" or "rejected" and that they will not be hurt.

Usually the counselor is able to establish such a rapport that clients can be directed to Al-Anon within eight to twelve weeks. It is found that Adult

Children more easily identify with the Al-Anon meetings specifically oriented toward Adult Children. It is suggested they begin there for immediate identification and bonding and that they go to several meetings before they make any decision or judgment about how they like it.

Because Adult Child meetings are so new, most members are in the initial stages of their recovery, so it is beneficial for clients to attend a "traditional" Twelve Step meeting as well; usually more long-term recovery is found there. These traditional meetings are where Adult Children find their sponsors.

When a client is actively dealing with practicing alcoholics (spouse, parent, sibling, child) traditional meetings are strongly recommended, for it is there that clients will get the help they need to deal with immediate problems in their daily lives.

Otherwise, Adult Children are directed to Adult Child oriented meetings, where the focus is primarily on Adult Child issues. Here, Adult Children can begin to understand how their present lives have been dominated by the past, can learn how to grieve the past appropriately, and can discover for the first time many valuable things they never had the opportunity to learn as children.

While many clients feel at home in their first meeting, they are cautioned that they may feel awkward. It is easily recognized that they are frightened because these meetings ask them to do what has been contrary to their sense of survival and safety…that is, talk, be honest, share feelings and rely on others. Clients need to look for what they can identify with and try not to focus on what it is they don't like (such as sharing problems with a group of people). It is important to try to ignore negative feelings about the group, at least in the beginning.

The most common reasons expressed by clients for avoiding meetings are:

1) "I want to handle my problems privately." It is understandable that the client feels vulnerable in a group of people. This is an opportunity to have them explore the disadvantages of having to cope and carry the burden all by themselves. This process usually helps to ease the pain.

2) "Home life wasn't as bad for me as it was for the other people in the meetings." When clients complain that they do not have horror stories comparable to the ones they hear, they may be reminded that the style of drinking and response to drinking may have been less blatant in their home, but that does nothing to lessen their loss or pain. Working with clients to help them identify the loss in their life and to describe the pain they felt from what *didn't* occur versus what *did*, from what *wasn't* said versus what *was*, enables them more easily to identify with Adult Children from more obviously disrupted homes.

3) "I don't like all that religious stuff." Many Adult Children who are brought up with a specific religious preference are not sure they want to have a Higher Power because, if they do, it will force them to acknowledge their anger regarding God as they previously understood God. They perceive God as having abandoned them and then feel guilty for their anger. For many Adult Children, it is easier to say, "I don't like those meetings" than to acknowledge their anger. Often these people have no faith in anything other than themselves. They have been their own best resource and they become threatened when the concept of "turning their lives over" to a Higher Power is presented. They often need help in exploring and discovering experiences where they have faith in someone and something outside of themselves. This may entail helping them

not to regard the world as "all black" or "all white" instead of being more flexible in how they perceive and respond to situations.

4)   "I don't like the ritual part when everyone says 'hello', when I say my name, and when they clap after I am done speaking." When a client complains of the ritualistic clapping or "hello" it gives us the opportunity to explore issues of acknowledgment. "I wanted to spend my whole life making sure nobody noticed. So if I do try and change, I get scared…I don't know how ready I am for such an acknowledgment."

By this discussion the client has gone one step farther and is now recognizing that he or she does not really want to be rejected but needs to ease into acceptance.

Many times, just the awareness of these feelings allows the client to feel less antagonistic. These are all very important issues to be discussed in the therapy relationship because they are not only related to the client's likes or dislikes for recovery meetings but are typically lifelong issues that perpetuate the problematic areas of the Adult Child's life.

This counselor views the resource of Al-Anon…and even more specifically, Adult Child Al-Anon…as an extremely valuable adjunct to the therapy process offered to clients. Clients who actively participate in Al-Anon move more quickly in their therapy process…they feel greater support and validation, are less alone. The experiences of recovery in Twelve Step meetings induce Adult Child issues that are important to focus on in therapy to surface. Members of Adult Child Al-Anon take risks that assist them to be more trusting, and they are better able to identify and express feelings. It is in these abilities so essential to a client's emotional development (i.e. to trust and to feel) that the Adult Child begins to undertake the therapy process and ultimately establishes a basis for recovery from the past.

Alcoholism affects the whole family, but the non-alcoholic often presents a spectrum of problems that do not seem to involve the drinking behavior of someone else. At first glance, the primary problem may appear to be marital conflict, blocked communication, acting-out behavior of teenage children, and stressors such as unemployment, financial pressures or psychosomatic illness. Almost without exception, family members who have lived with the complex effects of alcoholism have a well-entrenched denial system. This is the only way the non-alcoholic has been able to cope and those who have never "been there" seldom understand it in all its complexity.

Rather than address the peripheral effects already outlined, the counselor should refer the client to Al-Anon, for help is needed with the central dilemma of living day in and day out close to someone whose drinking causes or has caused distress to others.

Such a family member is most effectively supported by those who have learned understanding and found ways to live with the disease effectively, in short, men and women who make up the local Al-Anon group. The counselor should become acquainted with where and at what time this group meets. Even better, an Al-Anon member can be called upon to introduce the client to the first Al-Anon meeting. The counselor is then able to treat the client for other problems, knowing that he or she is receiving information and support regarding alcoholism. Al-Anon is not a therapy, nor does it duplicate a client/counselor relationship. It is a worldwide, self-help organization in which each autonomous group adheres to a set of guidelines for the purpose of promoting recovery for each of its members. Membership is entirely voluntary. Each group endorses basic precepts to ensure effective operation. A simple explanation of group functioning based on Al-Anon Twelve Traditions follows:

1) In unity lies strength. Individual recovery depends on group unity.
    While each member is free to express his or her opinion, group
    conscience is formed by the majority view determining the direc-
    tion of the group.

2) Common suffering promotes spiritual growth. No one member is
    different from, or more important than, another. Guidance is
    sought through belief in a Higher Power, an outside source of
    strength, which is expressed through the effective development of
    group conscience.

3) Al-Anon's role is to provide a program of spiritual recovery. While
    there are pressures to conform to other recovery theories or reli-
    gious views, Al-Anon resists by neither endorsing nor opposing
    these views.

4) Individual Al-Anon groups have complete freedom to choose their
    own meeting programs. This freedom carries with it the responsi-
    bility for preserving the unity of the Al-Anon program.

5) The ultimate success of Al-Anon and the recovery of its members
    depend on limiting the program to one purpose: helping the fam-
    ilies and friends of alcoholics. Membership is open only to those
    who have been affected by another's drinking. (Other programs
    exist for those affected by drug addiction, gambling etc.)

6) Al-Anon focuses on personal growth for the family member.
    Although interested professionals frequently use Al-Anon as a
    resource, Al-Anon's tradition of non-endorsement of other recov-
    ery programs means that Al-Anon cannot recommend profession-
    als in return. Instead, Al-Anon maintains a separate but
    cooperative relationship with professionals.

7) Al-Anon declines outside financial contribution. Support for Al-Anon's worldwide services comes from the membership itself.

8) No one person is an expert on alcoholism at an Al-Anon meeting. Professionals who are also Al-Anon members should share only their own recovery.

9) Al-Anon groups require only a minimal structure. The equality of members requires only spiritual principles and logical procedures agreed upon by the majority. Special "service boards" or "committees" are organized to serve Al-Anon as a whole.

10) Al-Anon as a fellowship has no opinion on outside issues. Taking such a stand could divide the group or weaken the spiritual framework. Each group must function free from concerns not related to the Al-Anon program.

11) The Al-Anon program is based on attraction rather than promotion. Personal anonymity is maintained at the level of press, radio, TV and films. Al-Anon's primary purpose is to attract members by offering hope and comfort to any unhappy and confused person affected by another's drinking. Al-Anon wants others to know that support and friendship are offered to any who feel they need help and come to Al-Anon to find it.

12) Anonymity is the spiritual foundation of these Traditions. It is a common problem that brings Al-Anon members together, and subordinating the individual will to a source of spiritual strength adds to the healing process. Other affiliations are left outside the Al-Anon program to encourage a greater sense of belonging among the membership.

The fact that family members need help cannot be too strongly stressed—they are deeply affected by alcoholism. At recovery meetings family members often see that, after many years of suffering alone, they have finally found themselves among others who understand and welcome them. They learn where their responsibilities lie. They discover self-worth: they can grow spiritually.

Al-Anon Family Groups have for many years played a vital role in raising public awareness of alcoholism as a family disease. Al-Anon provides the professional community with a well established resource for referrals, locally, nationally and internationally. Together, Al-Anon and the professional community can help families of alcoholics find stability and a new way of life. Al-Anon has some suggestions for working with family members.

1) It is beneficial to the counselor to know all he or she can about Al-Anon. Al-Anon can be utilized fully only by those who have gained a thorough understanding.

2) Experience shows that family members are more likely to approach a person with an understanding of alcoholism than a person without it. Many professionals have found workshops on alcoholism beneficial. Inclusion of Al-Anon/Alateen speakers and the availability of Al-Anon literature help to make a workshop successful.

3) Counselors may establish a list of Al-Anon members who will introduce a newcomer to Al-Anon. There is no cost to the counselor or the client.

4) It is suggested that the counselor follow-up with the client who is introduced to Al-Anon. Some people are not ready for Al-Anon. They may be turned off by a certain meeting, member or point of view they cannot accept. They need encouragement and a place to express their fears.

5) When making referrals it is necessary to keep in mind Al-Anon's Traditions. The program is only for those who have been deeply affected by someone else's drinking. There are other programs available for other needs.

So that the Traditions are not unknowingly violated, Al-Anon suggests the following guidelines for those of its members wearing two hats:

1) Attend Al-Anon meetings outside of the counselor's professional setting.

2) Keep therapy and sponsorship separate. A client or patient should not be sponsored; they should be referred to Al-Anon.

3) Keep on a personal basis any recommendation of outside agencies, especially any for which the counselor may work.

4) Do not assume the role of alcoholism "expert" in the Al-Anon group. A home group should be for personal recovery only.

It is urged that those in the professional community who have, or have had, alcoholism as a family problem identify and come to terms with this disease within themselves. Those who do not may be greatly disadvantaged in helping their clients.

Counselors requiring further information on how they may work with Al-Anon should contact their local Al-Anon information office by consulting the telephone directory. Al-Anon literature is available, as are Al-Anon speakers, for outside groups and contacts to which the counselor can refer a client. Al-Anon welcomes the opportunity to work with the professional community in helping any family member who may need it.

Al-Anon Family Groups are uncommon people who meet to share a common problem: the effects of the disease of alcoholism on those who live, or have lived, with an alcoholic. In weekly meetings, members of the fellowship share how they have used their program to recover from recurring symptoms of their own. Their willingness to discuss shared problems and solutions spans differences in sex, age, ethnic, social and religious backgrounds. From a variety of circumstances, they meet as equals. This self-help program of simple but universal principles led to their recovery and a satisfying way of life.

In the Twelve Step way of life there are no rules. Each member is free to accept or reject the suggestions of others. There are no fees for membership and attendance at meetings is voluntary. Anonymity is an Al-Anon Tradition: members are known only to each other.

The Al-Anon program is based on experience. For this reason, members will often invite those who are, or have been, deeply affected by someone else's drinking to go with them to a meeting as the best explanation of how Al-Anon works.

Immediately, the newcomer will sense a warm and welcoming atmosphere among the membership, which almost always leads to participation in an uplifting experience…at least for the time spent at the meeting. The ability to rise above the immediate concerns of life and to find a common experience is often how the newcomer first recognizes the presence of a Higher Power…the name given to the source of this spiritual change.

In A.A. pioneering days, close relatives of recovering alcoholics realized they needed to apply the same principles that helped alcoholics in their recovery. When wives of early Alcoholics Anonymous members visited groups all over the country, they told of the personal help they had received by living A.A.'s Twelve Steps or recovery. This helped improve family relationships that often remained difficult after the alcoholic had become sober.

Husbands, wives and other relatives of A.A. members began to hold meetings to discuss their common problems. By 1948, members of Family Groups had applied to the A.A. General Service Office for listing. Many troubled relatives of alcoholics were asking *them* for help. But A.A. was designed to help alcoholics and not other family members. In 1951, several A.A. wives formed a Clearing House Committee to get in touch with those inquirers and to coordinate and serve the then-existing fifty family groups. As a result of each group, the name Al-Anon Family Groups was chosen. The name is a contraction of the first few letters in each of the words Alcoholics Anonymous. The Twelve Steps of A.A., almost unchanged, and later the Twelve Traditions, were both adopted as guiding principles.

Alateen became a part of Al-Anon when the teenaged children in the families of alcoholics realized that their lives, too, had been deeply affected by someone else's drinking. In 1957 Alateen grew out of their needs. A Seventeen year-old boy, whose father was in A.A. and whose mother was in Al-Anon, had been quite successful in trying to solve his problems by applying the A.A. steps and slogans. With his parents' encouragement he asked five other teenagers with alcoholic parents to join him in forming a fellowship to help teenagers with alcoholism in the family. The idea caught on and the number of groups began to grow.

The logos of the Al-Anon fellowship each consist of a circle within a triangle. The circle refers to the Higher Power, which may be characterized according to the preference of each individual member. The corners of the triangle stand for the three legacies of the Al-Anon program. They are Recovery through the Twelve Steps, Unity through the Twelve Traditions and Service through the Twelve Concepts of Al-Anon.

The first legacy, recovery, guides the way to a normal, useful way of life, the second legacy, unity, provides a framework within which Al-Anon/Alateen groups can carry on their affairs in harmony. The third legacy, services, requires carrying the message, informally to a relative or friend of an alcoholic, and formally through the structure of fellowship as a whole.

There are many ways to gain strength, hope and health for those unfor- tunates who have been affected by the disease of alcoholism. Al-Anon is one such mode although many Adult Children have received the priceless gift of serenity in a myriad of other journeys and processes.

There are many wonderful books on the topic of recovery. Many are listed in the bibliography of this book. They provide one tool for help, and daily reading fills the vacuum of the codependent's soul...that place we try to stuff with others-directed happiness.

No one has ever suggested that living with all the complexities resulting from alcoholism is an easy undertaking! Why, then, the emphasis on an "Easy Does It" routine? Because alcoholism has affected the family's well being in so many ways. There have been, at one time or another, money problems, health problems, work problems, problems with the children in school, at home or with friends. Most families suffer the deep fear and anxiety that somebody outside the family will find out about or condemn them for all the problems.

Many who are deeply affected by someone else's drinking have spent sleepless nights wondering how to get all the problems solved, with one thought chasing after another in an endless round of helplessness and frus- tration. All too often, a resolve to tackle a single problem gets sidetracked by a new crisis the next day or next week, and then the same whirling thoughts, or even panic reactions, begins all over again.

When Twelve Steppers refer to "Easy Does It" they are not suggesting more action, they are suggesting less action, less frantic involvement with the behavior of others and, therefore, less frustration. In other words, they are free to set the pace of living that suits them, not anybody else, includ- ing the alcoholic. Now they are able to participate in activities with others that will provide meaning and comfort, instead of constantly repeating old patterns of behavior.

Members can learn how to make the best possible use of their time and energy, to "roll with the punches" and to really choose how to tackle problems one at a time. Further, they make decisions in the manner they think best and at a time when they are ready for it. Once they have grasped the principle of this great tension relaxer, they can begin to apply it elsewhere in life. Normal involvement with the problems of others can be separated from abnormal involvement. "Easy Does It" is the key to the difference.

For those who are no longer affected by the problems engendered by active alcoholism, this everyday phrase can lead to increased peace of mind. At first it may appear meaningless, until the individual searches out the tremendous significance hidden within. Not only does "Easy Does It" break the cycle of tension and anxiety, but also it releases the person from irritations that are a part of daily living. It is a beautiful, practical tool for smoothing out confused thinking and impatient, headlong words and actions. It is a resource with lifelong usefulness.

Although they mainly express it in different ways, everyone seems to feel a great sense of responsibility toward the effects of alcoholism. One will make good the alcoholic's promises to pay; another will cover up someone else's absences from work; a third may take the drinker to task by trying to "straighten him out" in one way or another. When this fails, the family member, supervisor or close friend feels very much alone and somehow responsible for the failure. This may lead to a redoubling of their efforts to obtain results, accompanied by the same sense of failure and the same feeling that they are somehow to blame.

The "program" suggests that there are other sources of well being for the alcoholic; such a provider may be God, in the Twelve Step rooms often called the Higher Power. Thus, the individual is not alone and not solely responsible for the effects of this disease. "Let Go and Let God" indicates that this principle is really an exercise in humility. Family members and friends do not have the power to change alcoholic behavior. No one can control the actions of others, alcoholic or not.

If friends and relatives will let go of their own often-misguided desire to help and allow a spiritual source to guide the alcoholic instead, surprising results often follow. At meetings, members will proudly share how they have refrained from making excuses, or covering up the consequences of the drinking, only to find that the alcoholic has taken on some responsibility for himself or herself by paying bills or getting to work. Even if "Let Go and Let God" results in the alcoholic's getting into more trouble...with the law, for instance or with the boss...the person deeply affected by the alcoholic comes to realize that he or she is not responsible.

Also, by maintaining a healthy detachment from the consequences of the alcoholic's behavior, others may be in a better position to act and think clearly in situations that require personal responsibility.

At this deeper level, members learn to appreciate that they have little or no control over the affairs of others and can only be responsible for themselves. Practice of "Let Go and Let God" leads to a profound realization of how frequently a Higher Power does intervene in the lives of others and how wise the solutions presented are. Most, but not all members actively seek guidance from this spiritual source for the direction of their own lives and for the lives of others, believing that it is superior to all the efforts of the human intellect and the human will. Such a person is able to maintain a sense of well-being in the face of many difficulties whether alcoholic in nature or not.

Many a distressed person comes to recovery believing once the alcoholic stops drinking, all the problems will disappear. What a disappointment to find that this is not so! What is more, alcoholism has been so much the center of focus that other aspects of living have been neglected. Many spouses have become so obsessed with the drinking that they have failed to monitor their own health or perhaps their own compulsive behavior, have not carried through their intentions to continue their own education or take that promised vacation. A young alcoholic may have absorbed so much of his or her parents' attention that brothers and sisters have been short-changed. The professional may have let other aspects of his or her work slip, or have neglected other employees.

"First Things First" allows everyone to take exclusive attention off the alcoholic problem and begin to assess the relative importance of all aspects of living. In admitting that responses to the alcoholic behavior are usually out of proportion to the situation, this clarification of the order of importance clears the way for more constructive living.

When members begin to focus on themselves, according to the principle of "First Things First", the self-knowledge that results places them in a better position to proceed to a life of order. If the decision is made to solve a single problem, the success achieved results in a feeling of well-being. The spouse may decide to get a long overdue medical check-up. A husband of an alcoholic wife may decide that his children need the care of a neighbor or a housekeeper while he is at work. A parent may decide that his alcoholic youngster may no longer be permitted to drive the family car. "First Things First" permits the individual to progress steadily toward recovery by choosing the next step.

If sobriety for the alcoholic does come, "First Things First" still ensures that the family or friend continues a life of serenity in the face of profound change. Rather than wondering how many A.A. meetings the alcoholic is attending or whether he or she will drink again, recovery members focus on their own affairs by continuing to seek lives of calmness and order.

"First Things First", in a spiritual sense, leads to an understanding that each person should concentrate on his or her own spiritual and emotional health in order to maintain a sense of contentment with life, rather than depending upon the actions of others, alcoholic or not.

The slogan, "Live and Let Live", speaks profoundly of relationships with alcoholics and others.

Al-Anon members are challenged to live a full life, despite the circumstances. They are encouraged to put aside all personal feelings of guilt, failure and recrimination and to find life enjoyable. In seeking a fuller life, many will reach out to one another by telephone to share in their search for a life of serenity and happiness through simple and attainable things…the enjoyment of good weather, a sunset, a chat with a neighbor or co-worker, a chance to be of service to someone else. They have learned the trick that problems seem to diminish in direct correlation to one's ability to put them in their true perspective. Others are blessed with a sense of humor that enables them to keep a sense of proportion about themselves and their circumstances. The second part of the slogan, "Let Live", allows one not to judge the behavior of others, including the alcoholic. Few people always act in a way that can withstand close scrutiny by others, and judgment is reserved for the authority in a Higher Power. Those who accept the slogan, "Live and Let Live", come to understand that tolerance adds to the quality of daily living, whereas resentment and self-pity diminish the human capacity to live joyfully.

Frequently, all that is needed to lead a more rewarding life is a change in attitude, rather than a change in circumstances.

Each of these slogans represents a particular spiritual discipline. They provide a logical starting pint for dealing with many situations. They are also easy to recall in times of stress. An individual's response to them can be used as a measuring stick in evaluating his or her progress along the road to personal recovery.

The Serenity Prayer "God grant me the serenity to accept the things I cannot change, courage to change the things I can, and the wisdom to know the difference," is used as a daily reminder by many in times of quiet meditation, or as a guide in moments of stress. Like so much of the Twelve Step program, it combines comfort, inspiration and practicability. The three key concepts in the Serenity Prayer are acceptance, courage and wisdom. Members aspire to these qualities in their search for recovery and growing emotional maturity. The simple repetition of this prayer means that each member continues to take a glance down the road to recovery to make sure that his or her daily path leads toward this goal.

To many newcomers, the idea of accepting the disease of alcoholism is not an easy one. Acceptance of all that is distressing seems like a sign of weakness. It can be argued that if a person is an upright, intelligent, strong or loving person, then he or she has necessary qualities to force a change in the alcoholic situation. Before recovery, many a struggling individual has tried desperately to change others by attempting to live up to standards that are close to perfection. Put another way, Adult Children my think that they can remake the alcoholic so that he or she conforms to what is expected of a spouse, parent, child, friend, employee and so on. Many newcomers enter the "program" feeling quite worn out by the struggle to get others, especially the alcoholic, to toe the line and do what is expected of them.

To accept that they do not have the power to make the alcoholic stop drinking is the first order of business for newcomers. This surrender to the inevitable comes quickly for people whose perceptions have been blunted by living with so much pain for so long. Often, the acceptance that someone close to them has a serious, complex disease over which neither the sick person nor anyone else has any control is arrived at only after much soul searching and sharing with other program members.

But once acceptance of the reality of alcoholism comes about and resistance to the nature of the disease is at an end, the road to recovery is made clear at last.

Sooner or later the member is confronted with a choice. Having acquired an understanding of alcoholism and how this disease affects others, what should be done about it? On the one hand, the members are surrounded by others who have come to terms with similar circumstances in a variety of ways. On the other, it is quite possible to walk away from a situation that seems unendurable.

Recovery asks that we not be too hasty in making conclusions before considering all the alternatives. Courage is needed to take a long, honest look at how he or she has contributed to the situation. It is not easy for the newcomer to admit that he or she has had irrational behavior, at times. It takes courage to extract the negative personal qualities buried beneath the confusion of alcoholism masking their presence, and more courage to be willing to change them. This can be done by not making excuses for their own behavior; or, without indulging in the human tendency to blame others. In this way, one develops a realistic concept of what they are able to change in the situation, whether the alcoholic continues to drink or not.

With a growing sense that much can be done to improve the situation, one can make a reappraisal of the alcoholic dilemma. With a quiet mind, unhampered by resentment or bitterness, he or she is free to make decisions in his or her own best interest and that of others who are close to them. The wisdom to choose rightly is sought from the guidance of a spiritual source...the "group", a Higher Power, or the God of our understanding. In seeking the right answer, the recovering individual experiences a lessening of reliance on self-will and an increase in discernment between what can realistically be achieved and what cannot. Frequently, relinquishing that which cannot be changed is experienced as relief and unburdening or peace of mind. This can be described as serenity!

A change is thinking and feeling leads to a change in attitude toward the situation. Acceptance becomes a source of strength and freedom and changing "the things I can" becomes a lifetime program. A deeper understanding of what it means to be human leads inevitably toward a source of wisdom and power outside oneself. They come to realize that they have found sound philosophy for living that reaches far beyond the immediate situation.

CHAPTER V

▼

CASE STUDIES

Serenity Does Not Depend On Sobriety

When I see a newcomer to recovery, with that typical look of fear and anxiety, my heart goes out to her. I want to express that serenity and peace of mind do not depend on a spouse's sobriety. I would like to spare her the years of anguish I lived through before I learned that my serenity depends only on me.

For the first eighteen years of my marriage, my constant prayer was for my husband to stop drinking. At that time I had not heard of A.A. and didn't know what an alcoholic was.

My husband has been in and out of A.A. for the past several years, but only because of my pushing and threatening. He went to meetings only to appease me and not to help himself. I felt a constant weight of guilt. Was I to blame? What was my responsibility in this situation? I had to do something, I told myself. I must pray harder, go to church oftener. Should

I leave him? Should I do this or that? I turned from one desperation solution to another.

With this entire scenario going through my mind, all I could think of was sleep…retreat from my problems. They were too overpowering. And I did sleep, by my own choice. I tried to take my life. When I awoke in the hospital my first thought was: God in Heaven, what have I done? What have I done to my children, my family…what fear have I put them through!

I owe my life to the help of "the fellowship", to our priest (who is a good friend), to understanding doctors, and to my wonderful and dear family. They were the instruments God used to pull me back from the depths of despair. The gift of life I received I compare to the gift the alcoholic receives when he finds sobriety. My gratitude helped me to make peace with myself.

Through recovery, after many years, I finally found my release. I took the first of our Twelve Steps, the one that says, "Admitted that we were powerless over alcohol, that our lives had become unmanageable." Now I accept the fact that I am powerless. I take care of myself and try to improve myself for my children, my family and for me. For the first time in years, I have begun to find happiness in little things. In the past I was too miserable to see things that were there all the time to be appreciated: each day has something good; the sun is shining, or it's raining and we needed rain; my children are well and happy.

Recovery is as necessary to me as the food I eat and the air I breathe. It is a wonderful help in facing all problems. They may be small or large problems that go along with bringing up children, perhaps an illness, the loss of a loved one, or even a great crisis. I try to remember that out of every difficulty, every failure, some good will come. Perhaps not at once, perhaps as a guidepost to the handling of future difficulties.

I often think that for us God may have some special purpose. Many who have tried to help my husband have become stronger themselves when they have seen what he has gone through. So, even in his way, unknowingly, he has helped someone else. Perhaps God's wish for me is to help other wives and families.

Thoughts of this kind are a great comfort to me. I no longer feel I'm deprived when I miss this party or that outing, when I can't go here or there. I consider what I have: my home, my four lovely children; I consider how much better off I am than my husband. He is the one who is missing so much, not I.

I must fulfill the role I was intended for. A wife, a mother, a member of society. I cannot do it as a self-pitying neurotic. I know that we are not sent more suffering than we can bear. This thought gives me strength for whatever may come.

When I first came to recovery I didn't know what to expect. I had the attitude: I'm here, help me! I thought I would find an overnight solution to all my problems, but I found that recovery's purpose is to show us how to help ourselves. Active participation in meetings, and plenty of reading, help things fall into place. Each day things become clearer to me.

There are blue days, of course. When they come, I say to myself, "you have no time for self-pity." At such times I have to force myself to keep my mind off my troubles. The best therapy I have found is to keep busy. I take my house apart and clean and clean. I lose myself in a good novel. I have my hair done. I buy material and sew. And I've learned never to do things "with a vengeance". I just take them easy and savor every moment of accomplishing something.

I don't look on our problem as a cross to bear but as something that has been sent to show me a beautiful new way of life I would not have known otherwise. I have grown more aware of people; I have an urgent desire to help them find the kind of serenity I live with today. It has made me grateful for little things I used to take for granted...the sun, the trees, God's creatures and friends. I am trying to pass this way of living on to my children so they will know how to face problems with courage.

My greatest compliment came from my 14-year-old when he said to me: "Mom, how come you're so happy and Dad is still drinking?"

Finally, my prayer is no longer, "Please God! May it be your will that my husband stops drinking," Now it is, "Please God! Show me your way and give me the wisdom and strength to follow it." Perhaps that's the answer.

I have returned to school and I am fulfilling my personal career goals in business management. I am a responsible, trust-worthy, competent leader today. I no longer focus on others' shortcomings nor do I try to control their lives, businesses, and finances. I am far too busy accomplishing the dreams and goals I have for my own life...a successful life based upon perseverance, "showing up" for daily tasks and acceptance of life on life's terms. Life today is an adventure and the journey is far better than the destination.

I Knew All There Was To Know

I don't know what made me look for a job in an alcoholic treatment center when I finished nursing school. Maybe it was God guiding me. Anyway, there I was...up to my enema bags in drunks! As part of my responsibilities I had to attend a weekly Al-Anon meeting.

When I was a teenager, a friend invited me to attend Alateen with her because I was complaining about my alcoholic father. I declined. I thought I didn't need help from any one. I knew all there was to know about getting along in an alcoholic family. That was still the song I was singing when I prepared to attend my first Al-Anon meeting!

I thought I knew what Al-Anon was all about. It was a place where people got together to talk about how awful it is to be stuck with an alcoholic. It also served to get them out of the house for a few hours without feeling guilty. In that sense, I was happy to attend Al-Anon: the opportunity to get away from the nursing floor was very appealing. But I was about to find out how wrong I was about Al-Anon.

The hospital-based meeting was held in the patients' lounge of the Alcoholic Treatment Unit. The Al-Anon Institutions Group was designed to introduce the patients' family members to Al-Anon. I recognized some of the people in the room as spouses of my patients. They looked a little jumpy and a lot depressed. I remember wanting to ask them: "What keeps you tied to an alcoholic? Do you love him that much? Are you crazy? Do you enjoy being a sad sack? Why don't you get out?"

I'm so glad no one was able to read my mind, to hear my cruel questions. There were other people in the room too, who didn't look jumpy and depressed. As I watched, they chatted and seemed relaxed, even cheerful, although to my mind they did seem a little smug. I was curious about who they were.

As I sat there wondering, a man walked in. The chatting stopped and all eyes turned to watch as he sat down and started to arrange pamphlets in neat stacks in front of him. I guessed, correctly, that our leader had arrived. He introduced himself as Bill and began to tell us about how he used to react to his qualifier's drinking. Then he told us about what Al-Anon had taught him and how his reactions to the drinking had changed. He described how changes in his behavior had allowed the alcoholic to become sober. I could feel myself becoming defensive. I had tried everything to get my own Dad sober and nothing worked. Now this man was telling us that the alcoholic is the one who needs to be given freedom? It seemed to me that the drunk is the only one who does what he wants and everyone around him is trapped. It never occurred to me that my Dad might have been trapped, too.

I left that meeting a little irritated. I wasn't sure why. Was it the sad-sack spouses? Or the bright-eyed "know it all" members? Or was the irritation caused by old conflicts coming back to haunt me? Was I still, after all these years, a sad sack, too? I was glad to get out of that meeting and back to work.

Sooner than I liked, I had to attend the Al-Anon meeting again. It started in the same way as the first, with Bill leading the meeting. I was only half listening when a spark of electricity shot through me and I sat bolt upright. It was a statement Bill made. He said, "Perfectly good people get the perfectly dreadful disease of alcoholism." My response was immediate and intense. I heard myself say out loud, "If good people can get it, so can perfectly dreadful people." I was embarrassed by the hostility in my voice. I was also surprised that my comment didn't bring about a hostile reply. My group suggested, in a caring way, that I had not accepted alcoholism as a disease and that when I did, I would feel differently.

I thought that over for a while. What was going on here? If I embraced the disease concept of alcoholism, I'd have to stop hating my Dad. How could I give that up? It was such a perfect defense against feeling hurt. I spent a good deal of time thinking about my attitudes and how they were interfering with my growth, not only as a person, but also as a professional working with alcoholics. I talked to friends and co-workers about my problem. They agreed I needed to work on this area of my life. By the time I attended my third hospital-based Al-Anon meeting, I had made up my mind to attend other meetings outside the hospital.

I'm beginning to see peace of mind in Al-Anon membership where I once saw smugness. I want some peace of mind myself. These members say they get it from Al-Anon. Maybe I can, too.

As it relates to my career, today I am a leader in the health care arena. The controlling I expended so much of my time and energy on, did give me the confidence to risk going back to school for a management degree in health care administration. It is amazing the number of us (Adult Children) there are in the "helping professions" and in the senior management levels of the Corporate World. "I guess my gifts and talents were always in the area of leadership…I just was way out of balance in the effective use of them!"

I Had Long Ago Given Up

In taking a close look at how I act I have come to realize how important it is for me to learn to love unconditionally. I must steer a steady course between the twin defects of strong dislike on the one hand and suffocating closeness on the other. With practice, I have come to grasp what is meant by loving and letting go. This principle sums up for me what I believe detachment to be.

When I first came into recovery, I had long ago given up any pretense at serenity, for my life was truly unmanageable. My son was an addictive alcoholic; one of my daughters was living with a similarly addicted person, and another was trying to cope with an autistic child. My wife had come from an alcoholic background, and I was recovering from the effect of a serious auto accident.

My understanding of the principle of detachment was at first rudimentary. I learned that I could indeed walk away from alcoholic behavior that was in any way irrational or harassing. I learned to be a "target out of range", so to speak. This physical detachment offered me a temporary calm in which I could get my thinking straight. But I have to admit that it did not help me with the feeling of resentment and apprehension these occurrences were apt to stir up within me.

Gaining strength in recovery, I learned that I did not have to leave the scene in order to find a sense of serenity. More importantly, I was no longer accepting the burden of guilt, which the alcoholic and other family members had been able to place handily on my shoulders. It was interesting that, at this stage, I felt free to pursue my own interests, both inside and outside the home. I became happily busy in new, creative endeavors.

As my sense of detachment deepened, I felt my attitude toward the program begin to change. At first, meetings had been like a ready-made escape hatch whenever the going got rough at home. Now I felt that my Higher Power was blessing me with a new family in recovery, and my sense of unconditional love became stronger as I came to realize that members of my own family were entitled to be regarded as in every way worth of God…given dignity and respect…especially to those who had unfortunately been afflicted with the disease of alcoholism. Continued involvement in the program, its love, understanding and support, was helping me to resolve my resentments, fears and self-pity. I began to realize that I could place this family of mine in the hand of a Higher Power Who really loved them, and I could go about my business with an increasing sense of tranquility and self-esteem.

I believe that my own growth in the program of recovery and my understanding of the principles of detachment were eventually helpful to my alcoholic son. When circumstances warranted invoking the order of protection the Family Court had granted me, the Court offered my son the choice of treatment, incarceration or voluntarily leaving my home. He chose the latter course. Now that he has taken some steps toward responsibility for himself, I feel I must free him *completely*, and let him go. Detaching with love and the continuing help of the program has helped improve our relationship in a way that is advantageous to both of us.

My sponsor and my boss have taught me to risk, again. Today, I am a case manager for a team of health care professionals who look to me for guidance, direction, support and even mentoring. I am a great listener, I know when to roll my sleeves up and help; and, I also know when to step back and permit my team-members' growth through their own consequences and behavior modification. I feel really good about my life and the contributions I make to my community. This is not a dress rehearsal I am living today…I practice living each day fully and can risk not having all the answers because my worth isn't based on "knowing it all" any longer!

There Would Never Be Enough

My mother's family were migrant farm workers and sharecroppers living in poverty and moving from southern town to southern town. She never stayed long enough in one place to have friends and rarely had a chance to say goodbye to anyone since her family usually moved in the night. She grew up afraid of not having enough and measuring people by the things they had.

We lived in a small town in rural America where only a few people seemed to have power…the doctor, the factory owner, the storekeeper and the mayor…and power came from money. My mother was in complete awe of these people and their families. She was a working mom before that became a trend, and every penny she made was saved because there would never be enough.

Some money was spent on looking good to those in the outside world, because they were considered the important ones. Our house looked good from the road, but the hot water could only be turned on once a week. My parents' hoarding made it very cluttered with old magazines, books and clothes. The only heat we had came from wood, and we didn't use that at night, so the water in a glass set on the nightstand by my bed would freeze. We never had birthday parties, picnics, vacations, or more than two toys at Christmas. Like many people, we had a nice living room that was never used, and we huddled in a much smaller room with very old furniture.

Whipping with a leather belt kept my brother and me on our toes. It hurt then and it still brings tears to my eyes. I learned only recently from my mother that her theory on child raising was, "You have to break their spirit when they're young or they will give you trouble later." I believe it worked much too well on me.

My parents didn't have any friends and my only friends were the kids I played with at recess. No child ever visited my home. I learned to isolate myself and distrust others as my parents did. I learned early to be ashamed of who we were.

I also learned that men weren't very reliable. My father didn't keep jobs very long because he felt he was smarter than his bosses. Women usually had to take care of men, I decided, and men could do whatever they wanted. My father drank and fought in bars during the war, but when he and my mother married, alcohol was never allowed in our home. They divorced when I was nineteen, and they both began to drink.

Somewhere along the way I believe my teachers became very influential because I can find no other reason why I decided to go to college. I dated very little. I was elected to many student offices and I never understood why. Someone must have seen something in me I didn't see. I was afraid that they might find out that I was stupid, or a bad child, but they didn't.

I didn't have my first drink until I went to college when I was nineteen. Then my ordinarily good grades and active school life disappeared. I had no self-discipline; my mother had always controlled everything. Alcohol made me comfortable with people who were better, richer, smarter and prettier than I was. Sex gave me love and affection. The first boy I loved and gave myself to drank and ultimately abandoned me. I was completely alone. I had no friends because I didn't know how to have them; no family because I wanted to be as far away from them as possible; no God because the limited place He had in my family was not enough to sustain me now that I was committing all the sins that would make Him angry.

I see now that alcohol and sex were my addictions. They killed the pain and seemed to be the only way to fill the hole inside of me. But they left me hating myself. Then I had to use them again to feel better.

I married a man I didn't know how to love. I don't know if he loved me; we communicated very little. We stayed together for ten years. We were rarely alone. We had drinking-couple friends. I slept with the men. I hated myself, yet I felt unable to stop what I was doing. My husband knew about the affairs and he told me it was okay as long as I was discreet.

After ten years of no commitment and no children and too many men, too many blackouts and too much pain, I asked for a divorce. I couldn't live with myself and I thought that getting out of the marriage would help me find what I needed. Within six months of drinking away my shame and loneliness, I met my second husband…in a bar, of course. We were so drunk that night, even though he came home with me, I couldn't remember his name. He was just as sick as I was and so he moved in the next week. This wounded man became my next addiction, my next god, along with alcohol.

No more affairs: my time and energy were now taken up trying to make this sad, hurting man happy. If only he could find the right job…if only I could help him go back to school…if only I were perfect, he would be happy and love me. I became addicted to his neediness, which almost felt like love…or what I felt like love felt like.

I allowed my husband to use me emotionally and sexually because I feared his anger and his leaving me. I finally supported him financially. Although I was drinking, my career was going well. Drinking was accepted there, and even encouraged. Over the next five years I allowed him to have all the money I made; I didn't want him to feel badly because he wasn't making any. He took over all decision making because I wanted to make him happy and keep him. In doing so, I completely lost myself. I took him home from bars when he couldn't drive. I let him drive me when he couldn't drive. I let him sleep with my friends because he wanted to and because I had not resolved my own guilt from the same behavior. I felt I deserved this and it would prove how much I loved him.

Finally, his disease became so advanced (with my loving help and support) that his bouts of deep depression, bouts of suicide and murder, became more intense. I became obsessed with stopping him. I would call the V.A. because he said he was in Vietnam. I would call hot lines to ask about him. I would call doctors. Yet I never mentioned how much he drank. I told no one.

I finally found him a job and we bought a house. By this time the good girl part of me had a good job with a big title and a lot of money. Somehow I had been given the opportunity to work and advance in a business that fitted me perfectly. Although my character defects…people pleasing, perfectionism, care taking, weren't working at home, they seemed to pay off at work.

We decided to have a baby. I was thirty-seven and now was time, if ever. During pregnancy I stopped drinking for the baby's sake and my husband just drank more. We brought a precious life into the hell of our own making. He was angry all the time because I wasn't able to take care of the baby, my job and him. We would have deep conversations (me dry, him in a blackout), and the next day I thought I was crazy because he said it never happened. Along with the depressions, there was now more talk of suicide.

I would drive home and wonder if he would be dead from a gunshot to the head. I began to sleep with a light on so I could see when he came into the bedroom; I was afraid he would shoot us all. He began to stay out all night or fly to Mexico. Still, I let him have the money. Still, I allowed him to pick up the baby from the sitter, drunk. Still, I allowed him to yell at our child and me. Still, I allowed him to control our home with threats. I had no one to talk to and no God except him. Insanity!

This went on until the baby was three then he finally agreed to see our family doctor for the self-diagnosis of manic depression. Neither one of us ever admitted that alcohol was the problem, even though he was now drinking over a half gallon of scotch weekly, along with beer, wine and vodka throughout the day. I had virtually stopped drinking out of pure fear for my life, but I allowed the guns to stay in the house. Insanity!

The doctor, who was a member of A.A., called me while my husband was in his office to ask how much he drank. My husband had only told him "a couple of drinks in the evening". The doctor told me to go to Al-Anon and to have my husband attend A.A. Of course, he didn't. Why should he? I was taking care of everything. I went to a couple of meetings of Al-Anon but I wasn't ready either. (After all, they didn't tell me how to fix my husband.)

It took another year for me to hit bottom. I left the baby with him to go on a business trip. Insanity! I realized that when I returned the next day. I was driving to work when an eerie inhuman cry came from somewhere deep inside me. I had come to the end. I called a hot line and was referred to a therapist specializing in abused women. She had no knowledge of alcoholism, but I did begin to attend Al-Anon and was referred to a psychologist.

I asked for help and suddenly there was help everywhere. I began to detach enough from my fear to see that there were choices. I arranged for intervention, which didn't work for him, but did for me. The secret was out. Although everyone knew…his family and his office…no one was talking to him about it until then. Yet he didn't stick to treatment or sobriety in the next year. I asked him to go into treatment again or we would separate. He chose to separate. I chose to get better. In Al-Anon I learned to detach with love. I learned that I didn't cause my husband's problem. I couldn't control it and I sure couldn't cure it. I learned that I played a part in my abuse and that I didn't have to live like that. The most important thing I learned, however, was that there was a loving God who was there for me, a God I could call my own. A God who wouldn't abandon me or abuse me. A God who would be there for me as my best friend. I learned that He forgives me and that He wants me to be happy.

The psychologist and I explored how painful living passes from generation to generation. We learn to abuse each other and ourselves. We also explored how my longing for my distant father influenced my attraction for unavailable men. We talked about how I saw myself as two very distinct people. One who was professionally successful and the "real one" who was not as good as others (the stupid, bad child). Together we worked to find the real me who could be successful in all parts of my life.

I have just recently confronted my own alcoholism. I felt stuck in my recovery. I had not unlocked every door. I had not been rigorously honest. The time had come. For the last year I had controlled how much I drank, where I drank, what I drank and with whom I drank. I would go months without a drink, but finally I could see that the need to control my drinking and my fear of getting drunk were not normal. My drinking never was. I had worked the Twelve Steps in Al-Anon with one big secret…my alcoholism. I had been comparing my controlled drinking with my husband's out-of-control drinking.

Now I am on a very exciting journey. I'm learning the power of being vulnerable, humble and honest. The learning that I am a precious child of God, and that I deserve happiness just because of that. I'm learning the power and peace of bringing God into every decision, every conversation and every relationship. I'm learning that the promises offered by the Twelve Steps are available, even to me.

I have a small business. I have a staff of two and I am the decision maker for the profitability component of my business. My management skills seem to surface when I need them most...I intuitively know how to handle things that once baffled me.

I have been trying to have an honest relationship with a kind and gentle man. We are both in recovery. Sometimes I can't be honest because I still have trouble knowing what I feel. Sometimes fear comes up and I feel like running again. Sometimes recovery is so painful I want to give up and find someone or something easier. But I know that what I have now and who I am now are so much better than in the past. I want recovery...God and the Twelve Steps, self-examination and progress, not perfection...for the rest of my life. I have learned that sex, money, spending, alcohol and relationships can't relieve me of empty feelings, a hollow soul or anxiety. One God has been able to fill me. And He was always there. I just never asked. Today I ask every day, and every day I learn something new.

Mid-Life Crisis

My husband and I are both Christians who are forty-five years old. We have two boys, now sixteen and seventeen. The story of my recovery started in 1992 when my husband, an auto mechanic, became unemployed when the car dealership that had employed him folded. What started out as a mid-life crisis soon progressed into heavy drinking, unbeknownst to me he kept his stash well hidden, and I was unable to smell the liquor on his breath? I did start to notice some bizarre conversations and actions. The criticism and verbal abuse became common over time, as did his mood swings. He was constantly telling me about my faults, "for my own good". "You are the reason for my problems and my behavior," he said. Although he was only physically violent on a handful of occasions, the boys and I became very afraid of his unpredictable rages, which were an everyday occurrence. He became a recluse. Yet I desperately struggled to maintain my relationships with other people. I felt trapped in my marriage: I didn't know if I loved him, yet I didn't believe in divorce.

Slowly I became paralyzed by guilt, fear and anger. I had always liked my job as a medical technologist, yet I could hardly get up to go to work. At home I couldn't function, except to do the laundry and cook the meals. In June of 1992, I shared my feelings and my husband's symptoms with one of my co-workers and she suggested that he might be abusing alcohol (her ex-husband had the same symptoms, she said). I went home and looked around the house with a more discerning eye. I found his stash of alcohol.

In the next six weeks, I monitored his usage. At a church prayer meeting I also blurted out what was happening in our family. Some people suspected it (they could smell the liquor on him when he ushered, they said). However, they never condemned him; they just accepted him and prayed. The pastor suggested that the boys and I confront my husband with my knowledge. When I told him what I knew, he said nothing. I then informed him the boys and I were going to get help, regardless of what he did.

The end of July, I started attending Al-Anon meetings weekly. I thoroughly resented being there, but I met people who helped me, like the gal who could laugh, even though she was living with an alcoholic. And that's what I wanted to do.

In the next months I remained open to anything God might use in my life: Al-Anon, my church, my family, my friends and my books. Al-Anon gave me a total understanding of the disease of alcoholism and its effects on family members; my church family provided Christian support, love and prayer.

I also began to realize that I needed other help. So in October I sought the help of a Christian counselor. He showed me how to cope with my husband's rages and we worked on issues of codependency, low self-esteem and childhood issues (lack of love, guilt and anger). I read more books during that year than I had in the previous ten years and I took notes on all of them; I didn't want to miss a thing in my healing process.

In March of 1993, my father died. In the next months my counselor and I worked through the issues that related to him. My Dad was a minister…devoted to God and to us, but he spent a lot of time with church members and was very strict and undemonstrative. I was a people pleaser. I was hungry for love. I found symbols of major events in my childhood…good and bad…and then wrote a letter to my Dad. In it I listed five bad things, five good things and five goals for my recovery. It was painful. I cried a lot, but it was necessary. I'd like to think that Dad looked down from Heaven and saw what was in the letter.

My sessions with the counselor ended in May, although I still attended Al-Anon, which I did faithfully for over a year (now I still attend infrequently to remind myself of my recovery process). In the process of it all, I learned to laugh.

In June of 1993, I heard a program in which a woman who attended Al-Anon talked about how successful an intervention had been for her husband. I started to think about this seriously and I began to realize that love is doing what is best for the other person, not necessarily what he wants. So I asked my church family to begin praying. I planned the intervention for August, just before our vacation so my husband couldn't use missing work as an excuse. I coordinated it with the program counselor, my husband's father, the boys and myself, and two men from church whom he respected (his employer declined). Our church family prayed the whole weekend before the intervention, that very day, and that very hour. Within one hour from the time my husband arrived home to see us all gathered there, he consented to being admitted to the treatment center. The power of prayer!

My husband was in treatment for a month, receiving all kinds of cards every day from our church family, our relations and our friends. (All the daily cards surprised the program's employees; they had never seen anybody receive that many.) The day he came home from treatment I gave a workshop on codependency at a women's retreat, with his encouragement I had set this as a goal a year earlier, as part of my recovery.

That fall was a real struggle for my husband. He had some relapses but I knew I had to let him work through his problems himself. Since January of 1994, however, he improved steadily. We were even able to have an exchange student in our home for three weeks of the summer, and my husband enjoyed him so much. What a pleasant turnaround!

Regardless of what my husband chooses, I'm only responsible for my choices, and me and I'm only responsible to God, not to anyone else. I have chosen to love my husband (I knew he had value all along) and to be committed to our marriage (I'm not sure of his commitment at this point, but that'll be his choice).

I have backed out of my compulsive church involvements; I'm being selective about what I do to serve God (being a preacher's kid, "serving" was all I knew). I am confident in my relationship with God, regardless of what others may think or do. Nothing can shake that. Does my husband meet my needs yet? No. And that's okay, because God does in so many neat and creative ways.

I am involved in management today. I am the office manager for a dentist. I assist with simple procedures, I take care of all insurance authorizations and I am the leader for a staff of seven. I am a good manager of tasks...I do not manage people; I let them do that for themselves. Truly,

God is doing for me what I could never do for myself; but, as a team, *we* are very accomplished.

The Sins Of The Fathers

My father is a recovering alcoholic. His father was an alcoholic and his only sibling is an active alcoholic. My great-grandfather was a very strict, religious man who physically abused my grandfather. In our case the sins of the fathers went into the third and fourth generations.

My mother also came from a dysfunctional family. Her father was a vagrant who had just finished hitchhiking from California when he met my grandmother. Granddad never worked more than one-year anywhere, and often went without work. My grandmother soon found solace in other men's arms. My mother lived in a small town where her father was quickly labeled a "bum", her mother, a "whore".

My Mom had two nervous breakdowns while the four of us children were still very small. Doctors treated her with "uppers" and she soon became addicted. When these doctors would no longer prescribe the pills for her she went to other doctors who prescribed them, the popular diet pills, which gave her the same feeling.

We never had friends come over when we were kids because we never knew when Dad would be coming home (if he came home) or what mood Mom would be in. Very early one morning, when the rest of the family was asleep, my Dad put something on the stove to cook and then passed out. He nearly burned the house down. Mom would often lock him out of the bedroom at night and he'd whine and cry like a baby. One time when I was twelve, I woke up because my whole body was numb and tingling. When I opened my eyes, Dad was on top of me, passed out. I remember how dirty and invaded I felt. I remember trying to shake off his touch. I lost all respect for Dad as early as I can remember and I resented my mother because I thought it was her fault he drank.

My older brother was the peacemaker. When Mom would start screaming and throwing things at Dad, my brother would gather the rest of us together and we would sit at the top of the stairs. He would always tell us to keep quiet and be good. My brother would also referee when the three of us fought. He was our parent. We asked him what we could or could not do; he always knew what the mood was.

The last day my father drank, he had been gone on a week's binge. His skin looked gray and he looked very tired. (I later learned that he had spent most of the week in a fleabag hotel, hallucinating that his room was filled with snakes.) Dad loaded his shotgun, announced he was going to kill himself, and then went out to the barn. Mom started screaming and he shot in the air, warning her to let him alone. I remember her punching him and then she ran toward the house, Dad coming after her.

My older brother had us huddled in the stairway. I broke away to come to Mom's rescue, just in time to watch my Dad cock the rifle and point it at her. She threw herself down on the floor and Dad stood there with the gun pointed at me. "Pull the trigger!" I screamed. I hated our family and him. Instead, he went back to the barn.

That's the last we saw of him for six weeks. Now we know that he committed himself to an inpatient treatment center. Then, it was a big secret. Both sets of grandparents came to visit us during that time, but no one even mentioned Dad's name. When he came back, everything was very controlled and quiet.

Even after Dad quit drinking, he and Mom spent most of their time trying to work things out between them. I was always going out of my way to win my parents' attention. I was head majorette, held an officer's position in every club in school. I was voted Outstanding Sophomore, Young

American, Valedictorian, Graduation Speaker and Homecoming Queen. My parents never came to any of my award ceremonies, concerts or games.

Everything was funny to me and I joked life's problems away. My parents could not see my emotional pain, or perhaps it was painful for them to acknowledge that we children had emotional struggles too. I tried to fill that void with witchcraft, God, boys, activities and awards.

Whatever a potential new friend or boyfriend wanted me to be; I strove to be; yet when the relationship intensified I would back off 100 percent. The excuse I used with girlfriends was "I like to be free like a butterfly, not lighting anywhere for very long." With boyfriends, I'd tell them, "I'm just crazy."

Then I found one boy who liked me crazy, wanted me to be crazy and, later in our marriage, convinced everyone I was crazy. I became totally dependent upon him. My senior year in high school I was anorexic and suicidal. I was 5' 11" and weighted 120 pounds. One day I cut off all my hair on a whim.

We married out of high school. Six months after we were married, he became verbally abusive at the same time I became pregnant with our first child. When he'd leave for work in the morning, he would mark a line behind the car tire, so he'd know if I went anywhere. Then he quit work and stayed at home. To keep us going financially (and to enhance my blue ribbon for martyrdom) I baby-sat five children during the day, served for a local clothing store on the side and cleaned toilets at night at three different trucking terminals.

My husband constantly told me I was ugly, stupid and crazy. He purposely did things to make me think I was nuts. He'd tell me to do something. I'd do it, and then he'd slap me and ask why I did what I thought he had told me to do. After our children were born, my husband became physically and sexually abusive. I tried to leave him twice. Once he came after me as I was running down the street with the children and he tried to hit me with the car. The other time he picked me up and stuffed us back in the car then locked me in the bedroom without my children. By now I wasn't allowed to go anywhere. This is when the bulimia began, again. Each time he attacked me sexually, I quietly submitted. Then he would leave the house for hours, sometimes overnight. Once he was gone, I'd eat everything I could find and spend my evenings throwing up. It felt good to me. It was a release of my anger, frustration and helplessness.

When he started to abuse my son I began to make concrete plans to leave. I looked up a women's shelter in the phone book and arranged a meeting with one of the counselors. They told me what agencies could help me financially and helped me to locate subsidized housing in another town.

Yet, even after I left my husband, the bulimia persisted. So I went into a treatment facility, which was my first exposure to the Twelve Step program. My counselor took me to A.A. so I could understand my father's struggles. They made me work side by side with a wife abuser and a sex addict so I could gain insight into those struggles. Most of all they encouraged me to get off my butt and work on me.

The Twelve Steps gave me the courage to sit down with my parents and make peace with my childhood memories so I could sincerely forgive and forget. My father wept as he finally (after twenty-six years) had the courage to ask me if he ever sexually molested me. He wept even harder when I told him, "No you never touched me." They are foster parents and now house two or three teenagers who have active addiction and come from dysfunctional homes. Dad and Mom have nineteen years of sobriety.

My relationship with Jesus is my anchor. If I lose that, I lose my recovery. In the place of bulimia, God has given me a new way to release my feelings, in song…not sad or angry songs but in songs filled with the truths of the Word, songs built on hope and grace.

As a child, my picture of God was this tall, white-haired man in a white robe that was too busy to notice me, and I saw myself as too insignificant to bother Him with my problems. Now He is my Father, my Confidant, my Comforter and my Guide.

My church is primarily made up of ex-addicts, ex-cons, ex-victims and ex-victimizers. Even our pastor is an ex-addict. He said someone once told him our church was just a "garbage dump". Our pastor replied, "Amen, and Jesus is the garbage collector!"

This church is my home base, filled with confronters and comforters. They encourage me to share my struggle openly and to move forward. We have Wednesday night Bible Study, which is along the lines of group therapy with the Holy Spirit as a counselor and the Bible as our guide.

Our pastor encourages us to get together in small groups and minister to each other instead of going to him for counsel. Often the Holy Spirit will prompt someone to pray for me, even when they don't know why, or He will prompt someone to call or visit me. We all believe that stumbling blocks are merely stepping-stones to a deeper, richer relationship with Christ.

CHAPTER VI

▼

CONCLUSIONS/RECOMMENDATIONS

The recovering dependents and codependents find, through becoming willing to go to any lengths to find recovery, the ability to intuitively know how to handle situations that once baffled them.

The Twelve Step program is a spiritual way of life. Even the first half of the First Step, "We admitted we were powerless over alcohol", is a spiritual experience. A person in recovery needs more than physical capabilities; he needs the use of his full faculties as a human being to hear the message, to think about it, to review the effects of the past, to realize, to admit and to accept. These processes are activities of the mind, which is part of the spirit.

The beginning is often blind faith but the proof of truth is that it works! I believed those who said they had suffered from the disease of alcoholism but, through recovery, were now enjoying mental and physical sobriety. The truth was there for us to see. Shortly I knew the truth from my own experience. I was not only relieved of the compulsion to control other persons, situations and things; I was guided toward a compulsion to live!

Recovery also made me very much aware by constant repetition, of the freedom of choice, and this is the human faculty of willpower. As time has gone on in the study of alcoholism, and in recovery, I have been offered and have used the opportunity to learn more about humanity by learning more about myself. I now realize that when I first said at a meeting, "My name is Linda and I'm a grateful recovering member of Al-Anon" I was expressing the first truth I had known about myself. Think of the spirituality in such statements. My name tells me that I am a human being; the fact that I can know it, think about it and communicate it reinforces my humanity and makes me aware and excited that I am!

This, then, became the opening to the spiritual world. With the guidance of the program and the encouragement and examples within the fellowship, I could begin to find out about myself and be prepared to accept what I found I learned in the fellowship; that if others could accept me and love me as I was, then I should love myself as I was, not for what I wasn't, but for what I could become. So I have learned a little about my mind and about my will and about my emotions and passions.

I have learned that I can be a good human being, although an imperfect one; that, when I consciously live in the real world (sanity), each good day helps to counterbalance the past.

My religion did not give me recovery. Recovery gave me a greater strength in my religion. The simple contrast between active codependency and active mental sobriety has helped me to seek to listen and to apply the good principles of living, and I am rewarded with much more excitement and joy than was mine before recovery and all its benefits!

By accepting this mental sobriety gratefully as a gift and using it willingly, I have become aware of other gifts available to me as a human being. To get the benefits, I need only ask and then use.

This is the crux of the program and the crux of living: acceptance and action.

The gift of understanding has allowed the simple messages from my parents, my teachers and my church to take on new meaning and soundness. With the gift of serenity, I am ready and willing to accept what God permits to happen to me; with the gift of courage to take action to change the things I can for the good of others and myself. The gift of wisdom has been given to me so that in personal relationships I may act intelligently and with love or, as it has also been expressed, with competence and compassion.

Now I am trying to grasp the idea of living "inside out". The Twelve Step way of life, "24 hours a day", the meetings, the experiences, the consciousness of change in my life and in those I sponsor, those I counsel and those whose lives change as a direct result of the changes I have made in my life…all of these are spiritual. (The result of spiritual beings having physical experiences, if you will.) There is the spirituality of the Twelve Step way of life, which simply makes us aware of our individual inner resources. There is not materialism…just spirituality. If we take care of our inner needs, our other needs will be provided for.

A religion properly is of divine origin; governs the person in the relationship with his Higher Power; and promises its rewards and punishments after death. A philosophy is of human origin; governs the person in his relationship with his fellow man; and promises its rewards and punishments during life. Twelve Step work is a philosophy. If we follow the philosophy of the Program, we can regain an understanding of our several religions and a new and healthier way of life.

Spirituality and recovery are an awakening...or is it all the loose ends woven together in a mellow fabric? It's understanding...or is it all the knowledge one need ever know? It's freedom...if you consider fear slavery. It's confidence...or is it the belief that a Higher Power will see you through any storm or gale? It's adhering to the dictates of your con- science...or is it a deep, genuine, loving concern for the people and the planet? It's peace of mind in the face of adversity. It's a keen and sharpened desire for survival.

It's a man or a woman. It's gratitude for every happenstances of the past that brought you to a moment of justice. It's the joy of being a young man/woman in a young world. It's awareness...or is it realization of one's capabilities or limitations? It's concentration...or is it an easy sensing of the universe? It's seeing a mystical power of good in each and every human being. It's patience in the face of stupidity. It's feeling that you want to blow somebody's head off...and walking away instead. It's when you're down past your last dime and you know you still have something money can't buy. It wants to go home, yet being there. It's a rocket ride going far beyond what your eye can see. It's looking at something that's superficially ugly, but radiates beauty. It's a young child! It's seeing a caterpillar turn into a butterfly. It's the awareness that survival is a savage fight between you and yourself. It's a magnetic pull towards those who are down and out. It's knowing that even the bad times are good.

When people look at you and wonder what's with you, the look in your eyes will answer them: "Because I can cut it!"

The singular thing is that spirituality and recovery cannot be given to a fellow man by word of mouth. If every man is to have it, then every man must earn it, in his own way, by his own hand, stamped by the seal of him- self, in his own individual right.

What has always impressed me about the program of recovery is the constant continuing challenge to try to recapture some of the true and honest rapture felt upon total surrender; that special peace of mind that surpasses all understanding.

I think there is a relationship between that feeling and our need at the time we were introduced to the Twelve Step way of life. Our motivation, I believe, is a combination of enough hurt and the grace of God...the gift of desperation, I have heard it called in meetings. Surely a strange combination! I would not know how to express it to anyone outside of the program.

For a long time, I had the idea that I must succeed, I must be right, I must be important. If I let go, I thought, then I wouldn't be anybody. Well, who was I anyway? Just a willful codependent!

Now I'm beginning to see that letting go doesn't mean giving up. It means opening myself to new vistas. The moments of what I would call ecstasy. I'm thrilled and I'm scared at the same time. I feel, "I'd better not enjoy this, because it's going to go away"...waiting for the proverbial other shoe to fall. It's so hard for me to say, "Okay, you've had a little insight. Just let it happen!" The program says, "Look, we've got some things to give you that are really going to help – if you'll slow down long enough and if you'll relax."

These are not things that are going to make me special or get me a better job or make me important. They are just going to offer me a way of life that is beautiful. When I say, "I want to know something about the spirit in me", you say, "Go ahead. There isn't anything to be afraid of. The darkness you may encounter isn't going to last, because there will *always* be somebody to help you. You *never* do anything alone!"

In A.A. we have found that the actual good results of prayer are beyond question. They are matters of knowledge and experience. All those who have persisted have found strength not ordinarily their own. They have found wisdom beyond their usual capability. And they have increasingly found a peace of mind, which can stand firm in the face of difficult circumstances. (1)

I have come to believe that the gift of mental sobriety...health and recovery...is what gives value and dignity to my life and the lives of those in these pages. It is this that I have to share, and it grows as it is shared.

END NOTES

CHAPTER 1

1) Combs, B. "Moving Through Unfinished Business: The Recovery Journey From Codependency", Lecture, Charlotte, NC, 25 March 1988.

2) Covey, S. The Seven Habits Of Highly Effective People: Restoring The Character Ethic. New York, NY, Simon and Schuster (1989).

3) Cermak, T. Diagnosing And Treating Co-Dependence: A Guide For Professionals Who Work With Chemical Dependents, Their Spouses, And Children, Minneapolis, MN, Johnson Inst. Books (1986).

4) Al-Anon Family Groups is a Twelve Step program based on the Twelve Steps of Alcoholics Anonymous. Al-Anon has but one purpose: to help families of alcoholics.

CHAPTER II

1) Beattie, M. Codependent No More. Center City, MN: Hazelden (1987). Beattie, M. *Beyond codependency*. Center City, MN: Harper/Hazelden (1989).

2)   The Bible, New International Version: Ecclesiastes 1:9, New York, NY, WORD (1996).

3)   The Bible, New International Version: Luke 6:38, New York, NY, WORD (1996).

CHAPTER IV

1)   Jackson, J. The Adjustment Of The Family To The Crisis Of Alcoholism. New Brunswick, NJ: Alcohol Research Documentation, Inc., Center of Alcohol Studies, Rutgers U 1989.

2)   Williams, Kenneth, M.D. He was on the Executive Committee of the American Medical Society on Alcoholism and was a Class A Trustee of Alcoholics Anonymous.

3)   Reddy, Betty. She is a consultant to Parkside Lutheran Hospital in Park Ridge, Illinois, since 1969. She has written many articles on family services and Al-Anon.

4)   Ibid.

CHAPTER VI

1)   Wilson, Bill, Twelve Steps and Twelve Traditions, Page 104.

BIBLIOGRAPHY

Al-Anon's Twelve Steps and Twelve Traditions   ISBNO.919934.24.9

Al-Anon Faces Alcoholism   ISBNO.910034.55.9

Al-Anon Family Groups   ISBNO.910034.54.9

The Dilemma of Alcoholic Marriage   ISBNO.910034.18.14

From Survival to Recovery   ISBNO.910034.97.4

Hope for Children of Alcoholics   ISBNO.910034.20.6

Ackern, W. Perfect Daughters: Adult Daughters of Alcoholics, Deerfield Beach, Fl. Health Communications (1972).

Bradshaw, J. Bradshaw On the Family, New York, NY, Bantam (1992).

Wegscheider-Cruse, S. and J. Cruse Understanding Co-dependency, Deerfield Beach, Fl: Health Communications (1990).

Cowan, C. and M. Kinder Smart Women, Foolish Choices: Finding The Right Men, And Avoiding The Wrong Ones. New York, NY, New American Library: Penguim (1986).

Dobson, J. Love Must Be Tough, Waco, TX, (1983).

Earll, R. I Got Tired Of Pretending, Tucson, AZ: Stem Publications (1988).

Friday, A. My Mother, Myself, New York, NY, Dell (1982).

Gordon, B. I'm Dancing As Fast As I Can, New York, NY, Harper & Row (1979).

Gravitz, H. & J. Bowden; with a foreword by S. Wegscheider-Cruse, Guide To Recovery: A Book For Adult Children Of Alcoholics, Holmes Beach, FL. Learning Publications (1985).

Hayes, J. Smart Love: Changing Painful Patterns, Choosing Healthy Relationships: A Codependence Recovery Program Based On Relationship Addiction Support Groups, Los Angeles, CA, J.P. Tarcher (1989).

Jampolsky, G. Love Is Letting Go Of Fear, Millbrae, CA, Celestial Art (1979).

Kuebler-Ross, E. On Death And Dying, New York, NY. Macmillan (1969).

Lerner, H. The Dance Of Anger: A Woman's Guide To Changing The Patterns Of Intimate Relationships. New York, NY: Harper & Row (1985).

Miller, J. Take My Hand: Codependency Workbook, Nashville, TN. Thomas Nelson (1992).

The Bible, New International Version, New York, NY, WORD (1996).

Peck, M. The Road Less Traveled, New York, NY. Simon & Schuster (1978).

Schaef, B. Daily Meditations for Women in Recovery, Minneapolis, MN. Hazelden (1987).

Siegel, B. Love, Medicine And Miracles: Lessons Learned About Self-Healing From A Surgeon's Experience With Exceptional Patients, New York, NY, Harper & Row (1986).

Warren, N. Make Anger Your Ally: Focus On The Family, Hollywood Beach, Fl. Health Communications (1990).

Whitfield, C. A Gift To Myself, Hollywood Beach, Fl. Health Communications (1990).

Woititz, J. Life Skills for Adult Children, Deerfield Beach, FL. Health Communications (1983).

Woititz, J. The Self-Sabotage Syndrome, Deerfield Beach, FL. Health Communications (1989).

Wyertzer, Relax, Recover: Stress Management, New York, NY. Bantam (1977).

ABOUT THE AUTHOR

Dr. Linda Tague has 25 years experience as a Registered Nurse working in both clinical and leadership roles in the helping profession. She has traveled extensively speaking on such topics as empowerment; time and stress managment; boundary-setting; and how to overcome the effects of addictive behaviors.Dr. Tague has two Masters Degrees. She has a Master of Science in Counseling and a Masters in Business Administration. She received her Doctorate of Philosophy in Psychology in 1995 from LaSalle University. Her doctoral dissertation was on the disease of addiction. She resides in Saint Augustine, Florida where she has a private practice and facilitates workshops and seminars upon request.

0-595-19902-X